Life Freshly

Squeezed

Motivational and Inspirational Stories Squeezed Out from the Heart and Soul of Life, Love and Loss

Dr. Mark McGregor

Life Freshly Squeezed: Motivational and Inspirational Stories Squeezed Out from the Heart and Soul of Life, Love and Loss by Dr. Mark M. McGregor

Copyright 2012 © Life Freshly Squeezed located at www.lifefreshlysqueezed. All Rights Reserved. Printed in the United States of America. No part of this publication may be reproduced, stored in a retrieval system or transmitted in any form or by any means, electronic, mechanical, photocopying, recording or otherwise, without the express written consent.

Life Freshly Squeezed and its logo and marks are trademarks of Life Freshly Squeezed.

The publisher gratefully acknowledges the many authors and individuals who have granted Life Freshly Squeezed permission to reprint the cited materials.

Table of Contents

Introduction and Our Mission: Feeding Hearts, Souls and Charities

Become a "Juicer". Share Your Story with Life Freshly Squeezed

The Power of Family
Twisted City, Tangled Lives ~ *Betty R. Cornett*
When Granny Can't Remember ~ *Maureen Perry*
My Brother, George ~ *Adam Henderson*
Powerless ~ *Diana M. Amadeo*
A Part of Me… a Part of You ~ *Ellen Hines*
Honesty and Accountability Really do Count ~ *Rebecca Carr*
No Need to Say Goodbye Just Yet ~ *Suzanne Kunze*

Finding the Silver Lining
Mentoring vs Mothering ~ *Lillie Shockney*
Answered Prayers ~ *Candice Becker*
Loose Gravel ~ *Blake O'Shea*

Late for Dance Class ~ *Cassy Fox*

Don't Open the Door ~ *Marlene Andreasen*

Hurricane Honeymoon ~ *Mara Suranno*

Will I Ever Know the Joys of Being a Mother ~ *Linette Boisvert*

I'll Be Seeing You ~ *Misty Mills*

First Love, Second Chance ~ *Francine Jacobs*

Sometimes All We Need is a Friend

Project Hope – Remembering the Past, Looking to the Future ~ *Russell Johnson*

Meeting Judy ~ *Norma Mitchell*

Who Will speak for the Children ~ *Patricia Rogowski*

I Love Camp More than I Hate Snakes ~ *Melissa Row*

An Angel Named Joy ~ *Grace Williamson*

What Happened in Mexico Should Have Stayed in Mexico ~ *Linda Harrop*

Chick o Stix ~ *Tim Nelson*

Enjoying the Simple Things in Life

The Surprise Wedding ~ *Janet Evans*

Live for Today and Don't Worry About Tomorrow ~ *Belle M. DuCharme*

Albert ~ *Mae Baas*

Less Is Definitely More ~ *Leah Weissmuller*

The Christmas Tree ~ *Emily Murphy*

Love Soup ~ *Millie Gaulin*

Motherly Sacrifices ~ *Jackie Tucker*

Tough Minds, Tough Bodies, Tough Hearts

There's No Way Around but Through ~ *Mark Rickerby*

Near-fatal Attractions ~ *Abbie Donnelly*

Christmas in February ~ *Teresa Perry*

A Shower? That Would Be Lovely ~ *Emma Skov*

Perspective ~ *Jodie Cox*

Uncommon Strength ~ *Theresa Carpenter*

Three Year Homecoming ~ *Linda Davis*

The Cost of Choosing ~ *Valerie Mayville*

Healing the Grief

Friends to the End ~ *Nate Mailey*

3 AM ~ *Logan Preston*

Nellie ~ *Olivia Strong*

When Terrorism Wasn't a Word ~ *Agathe Girard*

They Acted as if Everything was Fine ~ *Olivia Middleton*

I'll Wait for You ~ *Mie Hansen*

Momma's Sleeping ~ *Tyler Webb*

Ivy ~ *Camille Ryan*

Keeping a Positive Attitude

Sing Your Heart Out ~ *Mark Rickerby*

Be Stubborn, be Strong ~ *Diana M. Amadeo*

You're Not Lost until You Are out of Gas ~ *Bob Janet*

Rock-A-Hoola Dreams ~ *Mark Rickerby*

Weakness or Strength ~ *Author Unknown*

The Tip of the Tallest Trees ~ *Mark Rickerby*

In it for Life ~ *Aubrette Benoit*

On Looking Through Old Photographs ~ *Mark Rickerby*

Gratitude ~ *Mark Rickerby*

Our Family of Contributors

Introduction and Our Mission:
Feeding Hearts, Souls and Charities

Life Freshly Squeezed was established by Dr. Mark McGregor. He has been treating physical ailments in private practice for almost 24 years. During those years, he has had the pleasure of hearing about some amazing real life experiences.

Reading or hearing about motivational or inspirational true stories has always been something that Dr. McGregor has valued.

Having been able to help thousands of his patients find relief from pain, his goal now, is to give back emotionally and financially, squeezing out and sharing these stories with the world.

We strive not only to provide the best motivational and inspirational short stories found throughout the world, but also to financially help needy charities.

Every day in every corner of the world, very special and sometimes amazing moments are happening, ordinary

Share Your Story with Life Freshly Squeezed

The stories featured in our books are graciously written or contributed by our readers and fans. We affectionately refer to them as our "Juicers". They squeeze out the best moments from everyday life events.

We highly encourage anyone who has a motivating or inspiring short story or poem to consider submitting it to us so it can be shared with the world. These precious moments do more than just provide an enjoyable reading experience. In many cases, they help heal deep emotional wounds and give people the hope and courage to carry on during difficult times.

We read through all of the many stories and poems that are submitted, and pick what we believe are the best ones to appear in our books. The authors of the top five stories selected by our staff will have their photos featured on the book covers. Our authors are like family to us and this is part of our photo album.

The staff at Life Freshly Squeezed sincerely loves reading and sharing all of these wonderful life moments with you, our readers. Please share these moments with friends and family if they touch your heart as much as they have touched ours. Providing an enjoyable and positive experience for you, our readers, while helping worthy charities, is our primary goal. Life's journey is too precious and short. Squeeze out the best life has to offer.

Visit www.LifeFreshlySqueezed.com to find out more information or to submit your story.

The Power of Friends and Family

Twisted City, Tangled Lives

Betty R. Cornett

Just days prior to the devastating tornado that hit Joplin, Missouri, on May 22nd, 2011, we had signed a contract for the sale of our home. We were gearing up for retirement and were relocating to be closer to family and home...closer to Joplin.

I was sorting and packing in preparation for the move, which was less than two weeks away, when I received a call from my daughter, Elizabeth, who lived in Springfield. I knew immediately that something was wrong.

"Mom," she said, her voice shaking. "Mom, have you heard from Olivia?"

"No," I said hesitantly, "Why?"

"Mom, a huge tornado just hit Joplin a few minutes ago – it took out most of the city – even St. John's."

As she spoke, my usually steady-as-a-rock daughter began sobbing.

"Mom, it looks like something off the news over in Iraq or somewhere."

Elizabeth a St. John's nurse, was going to work medical relief as soon as she could get her stuff together.

It was at this point in the conversation my phone signaled I was getting another call. It was from Olivia. Without a word to Elizabeth, I switched the call.

"Momma, can you please look on your computer at the radar and tell us if it's over."
Olivia's shaky voice was barely above a whisper. "We're under the stairway in the house, we don't have any electricity and it's really loud outside…please, Mom…"

I could hardly get my laptop open with the free hand I had. I was shaking too badly.

Just about that time my sixteen year old daughter came down the stairs; she'd heard the news on the radio and was coming to turn the television on for more details.

She saw me shaking and helped me, with her help I got the laptop open so I could see if the worst of the storm had passed. By now the television was on, though, and it took only a second to see that the worst was yet to come.

"Olivia, are you and Matthew alright? It looks like the worst has passed. But there are a lot of heavy thunder storms coming. Olivia, can you tell if your house is still standing?"

"We're both fine. The dog is tired of us holding on to him so tight. We're coming out from the closet under the stairs. I don't think we have any electricity. Mom, why did you ask about the house? Did something touch down?"

"Honey, it's bad. It's really, really, bad. I don't know how the media got there so fast, but most of Joplin is gone. The guy on the weather channel is saying it's at least an F4 if not F5. Are you sure you're okay?"

"Yes, we're fine. But Mom something's wrong. There are sirens everywhere, helicopters going over…lots of them."

"Olivia if you still have a radio with batteries you need to turn it on."

My husband, a State policeman, came in from outside. He'd just gotten the call to be ready to go if needed. His captain told him the reports they were getting could be summed up in one word – devastation. The look of dread and shock on his face when he got a glimpse of the television was one that I'm sure mirrored mine.

Olivia and I talked only a few seconds more before she lost signal. Matthew, our son-in-law could text, but not talk, so via text messages, we were able to find out they were going to try to find the rest of the family – six sets of aunts and uncles, dozens of cousins, and countless friends.

Over the next couple of hours, Olivia and Matthew texted each time they made contact with family members. Most lived on the north side of town where damage was minimal and most people were unharmed. Others who lived in the more southern regions were spared serious injury, but sustained serious damage to their homes. Slowly but surely everyone was accounted for. Everyone, that is except Uncle Don and Aunt Marilyn.

The tornado had cut a path across the city from east to west, several miles wide. Don and Marilyn lived right in the middle of that path.

By now emergency crews and personnel had mobilized enough to keep people out of disaster areas once they'd been removed, and no one but emergency personnel was allowed back in. But those folks had never met Olivia.

As she and Matthew worked their way slowly through town, I received short messages.

"Pray! Everything is gone, and it will never be ok here again."

For whatever reason, just as they were getting close to what had been Don and Marilyn's neighborhood, Olivia was able to call me.

At first, all I could hear was her sobbing – trying to speak through the tears, but no words were able to come forth. Finally, I heard, "Mom there is no way I can even begin to tell you what's happened. There isn't a house standing as far as I can see. People are just standing there in shock, other people bleeding, kids are crying and screaming trying to find their parents, tires blown off cars...I need to be helping them, but I'm trying to get to Uncle Don. I don't even know for sure which way to go. There's nothing...."

"Olivia, don't. Just do what you can for the people you see and Daddy can call the troop office and send someone to look for them. I've tried their cell phone, but didn't get through."

"No, I'm not giving up. I can't. I'll call or text you later." She was gone.

Twenty or so minutes later she called back; this time her crying was almost hysterical.

"Mom, I'm here. But there's nothing left. I know it's the right house because the piano is still here and the picture that hung over the piano is stuck in the music rack. The car and the truck are both here, but the truck is smashed under part of the house and the car is twisted around a tree in the neighbor's yard. I'm trying to move things to see if they're here...Mommy! I'm so scared! What if..." She couldn't finish.

Hopeless doesn't even begin to explain how I was feeling at the moment. My daughter needed me on so many levels. She was a strong young woman, but was she prepared to find her aunt and uncle trapped in the ruins of their home...or worse?

She wasn't there long before the authorities, thinking she was a looter, approached her. When she refused to budge until they could tell her where the occupants of that 'house' were, they were able to find someone who confirmed that Uncle Don and Aunt Marilyn had been taken from the property with only minor injuries and taken to a friend's house.

When they gave Olivia the street name, she went running back to Matthew who'd stayed with the truck when they couldn't drive any closer to the area.

I spent the next three hours back and forth on the phone with her as she and Matthew went door to door, knocking, hoping each door would be the one.

At 10:03 pm, a tired, scared, rain-soaked and desperate young couple was close to running out of doors to knock on. I was trying to persuade them to go home; it was storming again and I knew they'd be spending the next day doing what they could to help the hundreds and thousands of people in need. But they were just as adamant about not giving up until they'd knocked on every possible door. As we were 'debating' the issue, they saw a house set back off the street with lights on in every room. Could that be the one?

Running onto the porch they knocked. The man who came to the door barely got a word out when Olivia let out a scream (we were still on the phone), rushed past the man and into the arms of Uncle Don.

Cheers, tears, and prayers of thanksgiving weren't lacking, you can be sure. The only thing 'wrong' was that I wasn't physically able to be there at that moment to share in the joy and relief after the most horrendous day of their lives.

After spending the night with their friends, Uncle Don and Aunt Marilyn (along with several other displaced family members) settled into Matthew and Olivia's house for the next two to three weeks. And while thirteen people living in one house isn't what you'd call comfortable, the love and support of family is. The tornado may have twisted the town, but no force was necessary to entwine the hearts of our family any more tightly together.

"A happy family is but an earlier heaven."
~John Browning

When Granny Can't Remember

Maureen Perry

My granny taught me so many things; how to snap beans, butcher chickens, grow a garden. She taught me to make bread, jams, and pie crust. And she did it all with amazing patience and unconditional love.

I never dreamed, however, that years later I'd be the teacher; reminding her how to dress, eat. and keep herself clean. The woman whose house was always squeaky clean would throw her trash on the floor and wipe her mouth on her sleeve. But I don't, so I pray each and every day that I can work around all of these things with the same patience and unconditional love she lavished on me.

In the beginning stages, the cruelty of Alzheimer's is the frustration it brings to the afflicted one. Granny knew something was wrong but didn't know what (or didn't want to admit it). It frightened her.

When she couldn't find her way from the back of the grocery store to the front door where she'd shopped for decades, she was like a child separated from its mother in the giant world called the shopping mall. But an hour later, when she didn't remember it had happened, she'd also forgotten the fear. In the earliest stages, when the best cook in the county forgot how to make one of her signature oatmeal cakes, it was embarrassing to her. Passing it off on expired baking powder was satisfactory to most, but not to me, or my husband and my children who were with her most every day.

I didn't want to admit it either, but to ignore it would have resulted in the unthinkable. Why her? No one in our family had ever had this dreadful malady. Hadn't she been through enough? She'd worked so hard all her life. She'd lost her husband at a fairly young age, buried a son who'd lost his battle with cancer, her daughter's cancer was in remission, she'd gone through heart valve replacement, a pace maker, thyroid cancer. She didn't deserve this.

She'd given so much to all of us her entire life. And even though you might think a large family is a sort of guarantee or life insurance, confirmation that you will be taken care of in your old age, think again. Everyone was too busy to be bothered. Oh, if you'd ask them they'd tell you what a wonderful woman she was and how much they loved her. But when she could no longer cook for them and tend to their every need, they quit visiting her and they never called.

Not being there for her never even crossed my mind, though. I'm no saint, but Granny helped raise me and she helped raise my four children. And because of that, I will be there with her to the end.

At this point, Granny is ninety-five and getting feebler in body and mind each and every day.

The woman who so often used the phrase, 'even the poorest people in the world can have soap and water' can't remember to bathe, change her underwear, or get dressed. She barely understands how to fix a ham sandwich. But that's okay. My granny has always been there for me and I will be there to meet her needs until she draws her last breath.

It's not always easy, though.

It's not easy when family members who do little (or nothing) more than make an occasional phone call, tell you they don't understand what all the fuss is about. 'She seems fine'.

It's not easy when family members do come and have nothing better to do than to tell me all about what *we're* going through and how we could do it better.

It's not easy when I have to argue with my Granny about why she needs to bathe. I can see the pain and confusion in her eyes. She just doesn't know...and yet she still thinks she does. It's not easy when I feel overwhelmed with all the other things I have to attend to, as well, and crave some time to just be by myself. But then I remember that when she's gone, she'll be gone forever.

One thing she never does is complain – ever. She's appreciative for all I do and can still tell me most days how much she loves me. And while she can't remember what day it is, what she had for breakfast, or if she even had breakfast, she still thinks of others before herself. For instance, one cold snowy day, she told me she was praying that God didn't take her until the weather warmed up. Her reason – she didn't want us to be cold standing at the cemetery. That's my granny. That's why I do what I do.

The one thing I do regret in all of this is not being prepared. Her income is not nearly enough to pay for home-health services and yet she doesn't qualify for assistance. Had I taken the proper steps in the beginning to change that, things might be a bit easier on both of us.

When it's all said and done at the end of each day, though, if someone were to ask me how I feel about caring for my granny, my one word answer would always be 'blessed'. It is an honor and a blessing to be able to give back a portion to someone who has given me so very much.

"Grandmas hold our tiny hands for just a little while, but our hearts forever."

~Author Unknown

My Brother, George

Adam Henderson

We knew. We didn't have to open the telegram. We didn't even need the telegram. The look on the face of the men in uniform standing at our door was enough to let Mom and I know. George was gone. I remember feeling suddenly ill. Very ill.

I hadn't been home from school any time at all when they arrived. I remember thinking some time later how glad I was Mom hadn't been alone when she'd gotten the news. I was 14; the only one left at home. But that was plenty old enough to feel my own pain and identify with hers. It's indescribable.

I remember putting my hand on her shoulder when she dropped to the chair. She was shaking so badly she had trouble getting the envelope open. I know she had to be thinking - hoping…. Once she got the envelope open, she took a deep breath, began to read and the tears fell.

Somehow I managed to do my chores. Mom probably insisted, thinking the distraction would help pass the time until Dad came home. Dad was a feed and tobacco salesman, and spent a lot of time driving from store to store, servicing his customers. There was no way to get a hold of him so he could come home early. We just had to wait. I remember feeling like it wasn't real, that when Dad got home, everything would be ok. But it wasn't.

Thinking about it just now, my heart aches for Mom all over again; I wonder how many times she went over and over in her mind just how she was going to tell Dad.

The next couple of days passed in slow motion. I remember my older sisters and brothers calling several times to check on Dad and Mom. It was especially hard for my big sister, Helen. It had been only a few months since my brother-in-law, Charles, had died while serving in Papa New Guinea. He'd gotten malaria and hadn't taken enough time to get well before insisting on rejoining his unit. He had a relapse and died.

Losing Charles had been hard enough. Why did we have to lose George, too? It wasn't fair! Besides, where was Luzon?

I went back to school a couple of days later trying to feel normal. I told some of my buddies-the ones who had family in the war. But in a town as small as ours, the news had already gotten around. People were bringing food to the house, sitting with Mom and offering to do 'whatever they could do to help'. When I told Dad's cousin, who taught at school, I remember her asking when the funeral would be.

Funeral? What funeral? There wouldn't be one-not for three long years. The United States military wasn't concerned about getting our boys home to be put to rest near their families. They gathered the dead, identified them and put them in graves thousands of miles from home in the same land that had cost them their lives. That probably sounds a bit harsh, considering that's not the way it's done now. They wouldn't be able to get away with that now. I know they did the best they could under the circumstances, though. Half a million is a lot of people to bury. However, when it's your son, husband, father or brother, that half million shrinks to one.

Even when we did get notice the body was arriving, you had to wonder if it was only a box. The letter we got said that George was buried in a military cemetery over there-in Manila (the Philippines).They even sent a picture of the grave. That wasn't enough, though. Dad and Mom wanted, no, *needed* something more. But a loved one's remains were sent only if you requested it, and since we were in the middle of a war, it wasn't on the top of the army's list of things to do. What were they going to do? Exhume the body? If they didn't have time to send him home in the first place, how did they find the time to go back and get him? So, even though George died on March 23, 1945, we didn't receive that flag-draped coffin until July 9th, 1948.

Like I said, I know it couldn't be helped, but watching Dad and Mom go through the grieving process all over again was agonizing. It was hard enough for me-I don't know how they did it. Getting that telegram was like reading it for the first time all over again.

In those years between his death and his coming home to rest, we didn't have any choice but to get on with life. Dad went to work every day, Mom took care of us and the house. I went to school, did my chores, had a paper route, and all of the things a young boy did growing up in a rural community in the '40s. But life was never the same. It got easier, but it was never the same. There were even times you felt guilty for feeling happy. But I have been happy. I've been blessed in numerous ways, it is important for me to be thankful. I know that George and millions of others have made the ultimate sacrifice for the freedom that we all enjoy. Nevertheless, even after all these years, there's still not a day goes by that George isn't on my mind.

"Death leaves a heartache no one can heal, love leaves a memory no one can steal."

~From a headstone in Ireland

Powerless

Diana M. Amadeo

About a million homes and businesses across Massachusetts and New Hampshire are without power. I shiver along with the rest of my State. It's 20 degrees outside on the fifth December day, right after an ice storm that has left us without electricity.

Rain coats the region in a thick layer of ice. There are trees, limbs and electrical wires down all over the place. Roads are closed. The local power company reports, "The outage has caused the absolute, most significant power restoration effort the state has ever seen. There has not been a storm before in recorded history that has affected more customers." The governor has declared a state of emergency for all of New Hampshire.

I wrap a second sweater around a body previously racked by menopausal hot flashes and shudder from a deep down chilled-to-the-bone cold. I could really use some hot tea now.

During any other winter power outages, a kettle of warm water would rest over the woodstove for humidity and warm liquid refreshment. But with the children gone and my husband and I alone in the house, the porch is closed off, and our new generator is in use.

This is the generator's maiden voyage, so to speak. It keeps the house about sixty degrees, the refrigerator running and a few dim lights that mimic candles aglow. That's about it. I tried to use the microwave to make some cocoa but after about an hour and a half the cocoa was still lukewarm. Guess the peppermint schnapps additive will have to wait. Bummer.

Being without electricity is nothing new in rural New Hampshire. We are a rugged lot, used to downed trees and power lines, icy roads, frosty air, feets of snow.

When the kids were small, handling power outage was a family affair, though. We would abandon the bedrooms for sleeping bags around the fireplace, tell ghost stories, giggle, and cook up some New England chowder on the woodstove. We lasted a week like this once. It got cold really fast for me and the baby but not the rest of the family. My husband had started back to work, the older kids were back at school where they could shower, get warm, and socialize. My toddler daughter and I were stuck in the cold. As the roads cleared, we spent a lot of time at church and the 24 hour adoration chapel, thanking God for the temporary warmth and begging for some heat at home. Then we'd stop at the YMCA and take a hot shower before heading home to stoke the fire and huddle before it. Ah, memories.

At one time, keeping warm in the winter took months of preparation. In the autumn, the children piled onto a trailer hitched to a tractor that my husband would drive to a woodpile on an adjacent acre of woods. There, father and kids would fill the trailer with logs, then ride back to the house, where the split wood was neatly stacked.

My husband was picky about this stack of wood. As he'd rearrange the work that was just completed, the children and I would venture into the surrounding woods and pick up the fallen twigs to be snapped and broken into small pieces of kindling. "It makes the woodstove much easier to light with dried kindling," I'd explain to the kids, who by now knew the routine and ignored my unnecessary explanation.

Running a generator is easier, cleaner, and painless. "We are not suffering," my husband reminded me on day four post power.

"We're inconvenienced. Prior to the generator, we suffered during power outages." So true.

Our generator is not powerful enough to keep the water heater going, so my husband and I plan an outing to my married daughter's apartment where power has already been restored. There we will take warm showers, use a hair dryer and eat a great home cooked meal. With the frequent take-out meals and visitations, we indeed are not suffering.

The computer is down, of course, so I take this time away from my business of writing and indulge in a little water color pen and ink. It has been years since I have had time to paint and draw, yet it comes back naturally. I sketch and draw a caricature of my husband and me in overstuffed chairs surrounded by grandchildren, reminiscent of the Pickles cartoon strip. The last time I sketched, these people would have been my parents, not us, I mused. With the TV off power and the house quiet (save for the generator roar), I work in the evening by dim candle light on a family quilt that was started and abandoned ages ago. It is peaceful and serene.

"I have become my great-grandmother," I say, rubbing my chilled hands together for warmth.

But the cold is getting tiresome. I again recite the mantra somehow getting me through these powerless days. My power is no power. This fifth day without electricity, a weary woman whines, accustomed to all the frills and comforts that modern life brings. How did people survive before electricity? Has power made us weaklings? What's going on in the rest of the world?

It's very strange not hearing local, national, and world news. I use my cell phone sparingly to conserve its battery. The local newspaper is without electricity, so we have no news outlet there, either. My teacher daughter tells me that the school will be out of session until the New Year. Crews have been working hard, but some areas may be out of electricity for three weeks or more. Teams of power companies throughout the region have come to New Hampshire to help us recover. While running errands, my daughter has seen power trucks from Quebec, Virginia, Michigan, and Maine, besides local utilities.

There are shelters everywhere, but you won't catch us in one. Ten years ago when the area was out of power for a week and generators were few and far between, we persevered. Two or three days of freezing temperatures are enough for most sane people before they leave in droves to fill up local hotels and shelters. For some crazy reason, we never entertained the thought of going anywhere. Even when my husband was out of town and strong winds snapped a pine tree that fell on the house, we held steadfast. A neighbor happened by and called out to my young son, "Hey, how 'bout we take that tree out of your house?" And they removed the tree. Just like that.

We lost four trees in this most recent storm: two pines and two maples. A lot of trees in the area snapped under the weight of the ice. These trees were uprooted. Perhaps global warming accounts for the record precipitation we received this year; perhaps it was just destiny. But whatever the reason, the woods surrounding our home have been mostly under water all year round. The root systems are shallow. The weight of the ice and the prevailing winds served to topple some beautiful, healthy trees. My husband is outside with the chainsaw making firewood from the remnants of storm damage. He decides to try and salvage a smaller balsam hemlock that a fallen maple forced down along with it. He attaches one end of a *come-along* to the balsam fir and the other end to a nearby sturdy oak. Slowly the pine inches up to standing.

On the opposite side of the house, one enormous pine leaned precariously at a forty five degree angle, supported only by two sturdy red oaks. The oaks were leaning, too, though. The sixty feet tall pine was set to fall upon the road – a danger to pedestrians and drivers alike. The tree was too big and heavy for a novice to handle. Road crews refused to take it down because there were no wires or cable in danger. Insurance refused to cover its removal. Being responsible citizens, we hired a tree person at great cost to take the tree down and to keep the neighborhood safe. Kudos to us.

    I stand next to the second story window and watch as my husband cuts through a fallen maple. The odor of burning hardwood tingles my memory. My man stands and stretches, then, feeling eyes upon him, turns and gazes up to me. I feel his smile. He prepares to saw again, but then stops suddenly and looks to the shed. He drops the chain saw and throws his arms up and cheers before commencing with a familiar little jig.

    I see that the shed lights are on, before realizing the lights within our home are now glowing brightly. Then I hear the generator switch down to a low rumble.

Our power is back.

"The happiest moments of my life have been the few which I have passed at home in the bosom of my family." ~Thomas Jefferson

A Part of me...a Part of You

Ellen Hines

The decision to separate had been a painful one. You don't give thirteen years of your life to someone (including working two jobs so he could concentrate on taking the bar) without feelings running deep. And when it ended, it wasn't that I didn't love Tim. I did. But he'd changed.

Taking the job in the state attorney general's office was the 'chance of a lifetime' he'd said. We would be able to set up ample college funds for the twins, remodel the house like we wanted to, take the honeymoon we'd never had... But what Tim had failed to tell me (or realize himself) was that all that 'stuff' came at a price – his absence.

Now, instead of family weekends at the lake and the twins' swim practices and meets, I found myself living the life of a single parent. Or when he did want to go out, it was to some high-powered gathering where I felt completely out of place. Tim insisted he needed to be there-even when it meant missing Andrea's and Amy's birthday. That's when I said 'enough was enough'.

When Tim came home late that night I was waiting for him. Trying to remain calm, I asked him what had happened to make him change so. I told him that the Tim I'd married would never have missed his daughters' birthday or any of the other things he'd missed lately. I told him how angry I'd been all evening and that I didn't like the person I was becoming because of the person he'd become.

Being the lawyer that he is, he listened and then gave his rebuttal. He said that he loved being in the political atmosphere of the attorney general's office and that this was his exploratory process to see if running for state office was a possibility for him.

I couldn't believe what I was hearing. You change hair dressers without telling your spouse. But you don't change careers and thrust yourself and your family into the public microscope without discussing it with your spouse!

"Tim," I said, my voice shaking and tears spilling down my cheeks, "tomorrow, after the girls get home from swim practice, we're going to tell them that you'll be living elsewhere for a while-that we need time to decide if what you want is best for all of us."

I went on to tell him how devastated I was that he'd not thought to even ask me what I thought or how I felt. To that, he replied that I certainly hadn't complained about the things the money was buying now and that he thought I was being childish.

"If you want me to leave, I'll leave. Glen and Toni have invited a few of us from the office to their lake house. I'll be gone for three or four days."

"No, Tim. Not three or four days. I want a separation."

"Whatever you want, Ellen". And with that he walked out of the bedroom, out the back door, and was gone.

The girls were strangely quiet the next morning. They didn't ask where Tim was. I didn't volunteer anything, since I didn't know for sure that he wouldn't be back to talk to them with me. But when I hadn't heard from him later that evening, I told them what was taking place and that I wasn't comfortable with them or myself being in the middle of all that. So for that reason, he wasn't going to be living with us for a while.

They were naturally upset and had lots of questions. And were incredibly sweet and considerate when asking me how I felt; if I was okay.

The next few days passed with surprising peace. It was strange not seeing Tim at all, but lately he'd been around so little over the past year that sadly, we noticed very little change.

When I finally heard from Tim, he was calling to say he was coming by to get his passport and some other things.

His being in the house was strangely awkward. A little small talk about the girls' swimming and his father's upcoming surgery and his trip to the UK with three other lawyers.

I couldn't help myself. "Tim, are you…"

"No, Ellen. There's no one else. Ellen, you're the one who asked me to leave. This isn't about someone else. This is about your not wanting to be a part of my dreams."

"No, Tim, this IS about not being a part of your dreams."

Less than twenty-four hours later my phone rang. "Mrs. Hines, this is the state police. I'm sorry to tell you there's been an accident. Your husband was listed as a passenger on a commuter plane that reportedly went down in a field. Do you know if this is correct?"

"Yes," I stammered. "Is he…is he alive?"

"Mrs. Hines, we're sending someone to bring you to the station so that you'll be able to make any necessary identification."

I'd been in the lounge of the police station almost an hour when another officer came in and said that the plane had been found. He said there were two survivors and three fatalities. He was taking me to the hospital to make a positive identification.

Tim was thankfully one of the survivors, but needed surgery as soon as possible. His upper body was crushed and he was bleeding internally-most likely due to severe injury to his liver. He'd also suffered severe burns.

Tim and I had met in college at the blood bank. We're both AB+. So I quickly volunteered to donate blood to replenish Tim's system.

In the months that followed, Tim underwent surgeries to repair his liver and endured excruciating pain in the treatment and recovery of his burns. But through it all, Tim became Tim again. He laughed, teased the girls, and when I leaned over him to get his water bottle, he kissed me.

We sat and talked about the sea of emotions and experienced we'd been sailing since the crash. Tim admitted that when he'd left the house the day before the crash, he'd realized how shallow and empty his life had become. Before he'd turned out of the driveway, he had decided that he was going to ask my forgiveness and come home – physically and emotionally – as soon as he got back from the trip overseas.

"Besides," he teased, "you're pretty handy to have around. I never know when I'm gonna need you to fill up my tank again."

"You don't choose your family. They are God's gift to you, as you are to them." ~Desmond Tutu

Honesty and Accountability Really Do Count

Rebecca Carr

In our small community, news travels fast. And if the 'news' is more like gossip, fast equals the speed of light. Such was the case with Brent and Vanessa's marital problems. Yes, it was true – Brent had been having an affair with his receptionist. It was also true the affair had been going on for quite some time. The 'other woman' had left her husband of seventeen years and two teenage daughters with the expectation of marrying Brent and living happily ever after. But just because it was true, that didn't make it any less hurtful to Vanessa and her boys, or for the other woman's family.

While this certainly wasn't the first divorce to hit the local 'airwaves', it did take most of us completely by surprise. Brent and Vanessa seemed to have it all together. They were active in our church and from all indications, their faith seemed sincere.

Because the other couple involved had split as soon as the affair had been exposed, most of us expected Brent and Vanessa to separate as well. But we didn't expect what actually happened.

The Sunday following the 'exposure', Brent and Vanessa, along with their two boys, came into church just as the service was starting. And while they both looked sad and completely exhausted, the rage and humiliation you would expect to see on their faces just wasn't there. Seeing them there together was surprise enough. But what happened at the end of the service was beyond anyone's comprehension. It will stay with me for the rest of my life.

The preacher was making his final comments, and asked us to stand to sing the final hymn. As we did, Brent made his way down the aisle to stand up front beside the preacher. They spoke quietly for a moment or two before Brent sat down in the front row-waiting. When the song ended, the preacher announced that Brent had something he needed to share with the rest of the congregation.

As Brent stood up and faced each of us, he was trembling. He looked as if he had the weight of the world resting on his shoulders. But taking a deep breath to try and steady his voice, with steady eyes on us all, he began to speak. He admitted that the rumors were true-he'd been unfaithful to his wife and family. He gave no excuses to try to justify what he'd done. He laid no blame on Vanessa for what had happened. Instead, he gave her nothing but praise for being a loving, beautiful, and exemplary wife and mother. What had happened was the result of weakness and stupidity on his part. He blamed no one but himself.

As I sat listening to Brent, I was impressed at his honesty. It took a lot of courage to do what he was doing, but he went on.

"I've asked Vanessa to forgive me and for another chance to be the husband she deserves. She's said 'yes', and so I'm asking that you also forgive me. I've not only hurt myself and my family, but I've hurt you-my friends. I've betrayed your trust in me, and I know that's not something easily fixed. I'm asking for your forgiveness and your help."

At this point, Vanessa joined him up front. Together, they asked for our support and understanding as they worked to put their lives and marriage back together.

There wasn't anyone in that building whose heart was unchanged. Their commitment to righting such a wrong was brave and tenacious. Unfortunately, it is also decidedly rare.

A few weeks later, I had the privilege of singing at a ceremony in which Brent and Vanessa renewed their marriage vows. Never had I seen a more radiant couple. This was a couple who knew, in the deepest sense, how important their vows were.

It's been twenty-five years since the news of Brent and Vanessa's troubles hit the town. Today, they are still happily married. They are also proud grandparents of three beautiful grandchildren, enjoying retirement, and celebrating each and every day that they took the road less traveled...arriving at their destination together.

Within those twenty-five years, several people have come and gone from our little community, people have found plenty to talk about and still aren't always as astute as they should be when trying to distinguish between news and gossip. But you can be sure that there's one 'news flash' we'll never forget. And that's the one that really does end with '...and they're living happily ever after'.

"He who cannot forgive others destroys the bridge over which he himself must pass."

~George Herbert

No Need to Say Goodbye Just Yet
Suzanne Kunze

My Granny, in the early stages of Alzheimer's, was becoming more and more dependent on me. I didn't mind, though.

Twice a day, I'd go by her apartment in the senior citizen's complex to make sure that she took her medicine and ate her meals. I did the grocery shopping, cleaning, and laundry. I took her to her doctor appointments.

To hear her talk, she still lived independently. And she did, technically. Practically speaking, though, she depended on the assistance I was only too happy to give.

On this particular day, I'd been there in the morning and had talked to her around noon. She'd not acted any different than what was normal, so I was taken off guard by the phone call I received late in the afternoon.

"I think I'm having a heart attack. I need you."

"Granny, what makes you think that? Are you in pain?"

"Yes, I've been hurting all day and can't catch my breath. It hurts when I try to."

"Okay, Granny, I'll be right there."

I ran out the back door and across the yard to the field where both my husband and youngest daughter were on tractors mowing the pasture. After telling my husband where I was going, I got in the car and headed for Granny's. It took only a few minutes to get there, get her into the car, and start for the hospital. I did take the time to assess her condition; pulse normal, skin color good, temperature seemed normal...but she was definitely uncomfortable.

On the way, I asked her why she hadn't mentioned that she was feeling bad earlier. She said she didn't want to worry me. Then she went on to say that it was okay with her if she died. After all, she was ninety-one and ready to go. Actually, she was ninety-three. Then she said something that made me laugh, in spite of the seriousness of the situation.

"I'm glad it's warm outside. I want to die when it's warm outside so you don't have to stand out in the cold at the cemetery. I don't want you catching a cold or getting pneumonia because of me."

"Granny, just hang on, we're almost to the hospital. And thanks, I don't particularly want pneumonia either."

"You're a good girl," she said. "I don't know what I would have done without you all these years. But it's okay if I don't make it. You hear? You'll be fine without me."

"Granny, I understand why you feel the way you do. And I know I'll be okay no matter what, but I'm still not quite ready to let you go."

I had to smile to myself. There we were in the car, saying our goodbyes as calmly as if we were ordering something in the drive-thru at Wendy's. It was really rather sweet – in a weird sort of way.

I was pulling into the ER entrance of the hospital at this point, so I stopped talking, parked under the canopy and went in to tell the receptionist why I was there.

They quickly got a chair, helped me get Granny inside, and immediately took us to a room. They started hooking her up to a monitor. They handed me a gown and asked that I get her into it as quickly as possible while they notified the doctor.

I helped Granny unbutton her blouse and was taking her arm out of the sleeve when I saw the reason for her discomfort. Her entire left side was black and blue.

"Granny," I asked, "did you fall?"

"I'm not sure, did I?" she asked.

"Granny, I need you to think really hard. Do you remember being on the floor or falling last night or this morning?" I must have sounded less patient than I normally am, because she looked at me like a child who'd just been scolded. I immediately felt bad and gave her a little hug.

"I fell last night," she said as matter-of-factly as if she'd been talking about what day of the week it was. "I got up to go to bed and must have got up too fast. I felt real dizzy and then the next thing you know I was on the floor. It took a while, but I crawled over to my chair and pulled myself up."

"Why didn't you call me? Or tell me earlier?"

"I guess I didn't remember or think it was important."

"Granny, these people think you're having a heart attack because that's what you told me you thought was wrong. I have to go talk to them."

"Heart attack? I'm not having a heart attack. I'm having a bit of trouble getting my breath, but I'm okay."

I smiled, kissed her on the head, and told her I'd be back shortly. Then I went to find the nurse and explain the situation. She smiled and said she understood, but said that the doctor would still need to examine my grandmother before she could leave. I was fine with that, even though I didn't look forward to the lecture I knew would be coming about her being allowed to live 'on her own'. He wasn't going to be telling me anything I didn't know, but he also didn't know Granny.

Sure enough we got the lecture. I smiled, nodded, and said I understood. We were dealing with the situation as we saw fit.

Granny, on the other hand, told the doctor he had no business trying to tell me what to do; that I was the best girl anyone could ever ask for and that we were doing just fine without him putting in his two cents. Then I got Granny dressed and took her home.

Granny is ninety-five now and in the mid-to-late stages of Alzheimer's. We're still a team, but now she's with me all the time. And as long as I'm able, I'll continue to care for her so that when it is time to say goodbye, I'll be there to do so- no matter how cold it might be outside.

"'Ohana means family - no one gets left behind, and no one is ever forgotten."
~Chris Sanders and Dean DeBlois, Lilo & Stitch

Finding the Silver Lining

Mentoring vs Mothering

Lillie Shockney

You may not know the influence you are having on a young person until many years later. In some cases, you may never know.

When I was originally diagnosed with breast cancer, my daughter was only twelve. I wanted to be strong for her, but I also needed to take care of my own emotional well being. It was a dual challenge.

I look back on that time, though, and I thank heavens it turned out okay.

Today, I educate newly diagnosed breast cancer patients about this issue and the fact that their children are learning from them—learning how to handle a crisis, learning how to become empowered, learning how to juggle medical care needs with family needs, and learning to be a fighter.

I also knew that how I coped with the loss of both of my breasts (left one in 1992 and the right one in 1994) would potentially influence my daughter's self image, her sexuality, and her femininity.

She wrote me a poem that was read to me in the recovery room by my husband after my first mastectomy. It read as follows:

Appearance

Nobody's perfect
Just look at me
But if you really think about it
Who wants to be?

Beauty and glamour
Are nice to get
But it's what's inside that counts
We must never forget

I hope you understand
What I've been trying to say
I hope you get well soon
And I love you more each day.

Love, Laura

A decade later, at the age of twenty-two, Laura was interviewed about breast cancer on a local radio station. The interviewer asked, "Are you worried that one day you will get breast cancer too?" She responded, "Not worried really. After all, my mother showed me how to beat it. Actually, she showed me twice so I wouldn't forget." That day, Laura's words were proof to me that we constantly serve as a mentor for the next generation, whether we realize it or not, even when we are coping with a major crisis of our own.

"The art of living lies less in eliminating our troubles than in growing with them."
~Bernard M. Baruch

Answered Prayers

Candice Becker

My life was on a downward spiral. In just a matter of weeks, I lost my husband, my home, and my job. Everything I had been working for since my child was born had quickly disappeared.

My moral dilemma about marriage was taking a toll on me. I grew up in a very abusive home and the only good and decent things that my parents taught me were: (1) once you're married, you're married for better or worse, and (2) you work to earn your living, no matter what happens or how sick you may be.

When my husband cheated, because of what my parents had taught me, I forgave, repeatedly and couldn't bring myself to think of ending the relationship. It wasn't until I read a passage in the Bible that I actually came to terms with my husband's infidelity and acknowledge that it was morally appropriate for me to divorce him.

When my divorce was finalized, though, on the date of our ten year wedding anniversary, I went into a kind of mental tailspin.

I thought about the way he just left me holding the bag for a bad choice made, how he could cheat and still say that he loved me. I lost my job for the choice we made together and ended up in jail. He accepted no responsibility for any of his actions. Combine all of this with having to hold my head up and raise my nine-year-old son, who knew the details of his father's indiscretions, quickly sent me over the edge.

I turned to a close friend, who, at that time, said, "Hey, I know what you need!" He proceeded to dump a mound of white powder on the table.

"Come on, once won't hurt you. It will help you to relax and deal with things until you get it all figured out!"

Now I knew exactly what it was and I had done it back in my teenage years, with absolutely no problems. This time was different, though. I guess I had grown too weak mentally to deal with all of my issues any more.

One thing led to another and before I knew it, I was a raging addict. I was dealing, stealing, and using whatever I could get my hands on. I had progressed from snorting to shooting up. I no longer cared about what happened to me, what people thought of me, or what they'd done to me.

It wasn't until my uncle called me out for writing bad checks on my grandfather that I stopped and thought about what I was actually doing to the people around me.

My grandfather, God rest his soul, was the only person in my life that had ever truly cared about me. He was there when I was fifteen to help me divorce my parents and become emancipated. He knew about the abuse I had suffered and that I had attempted to kill myself. This time, he was there when I lost my job and became divorced; he gave me a place to live for my son and myself. He always tried to talk to me through every rough patch in my life but this time I shut him out, thinking it was best just to live in my own world. Boy, was I wrong!

After my uncle called my attention to what a dreadful, conniving addict I had become, I started trying to get off drugs. It was the hardest thing I had ever encountered in my life. I had no self-control and no will power. At that time, I didn't know that I needed something more. I thought, if I cut back and prayed as I stuck a needle in my veins, God would take it all away. I did this for at least a year. I shot up and prayed every time I put a needle anywhere in my body.

I eventually gave up praying for intervention. I thought, as long as I prayed to God, he would magically take my addiction from me. I never really tried to stop, unless I was out of dope for that day. I made it three days one time with no drugs. I quickly found out, God had not taken my addiction, so there I went again and still prayed as I shot up. I thought that God was never going to answer and help me.

One day, I'm at a dealing friend's house when boom...BUSTED... and off to jail I go! While there, I speak to a judge, who informs me that my only way out is to accept a new program for recovery and my charges would be dismissed upon completion of the two-year treatment program. The program was called Drug Court.   Thinking it was my quickest way out, I accepted after spending seven days locked in a two-man cell with three other women. I had no idea what lay ahead of me. I thought that I could get out, go to this program a few days, and go back to my addicted life, waiting for God to answer me and take away my addiction without any withdrawals or repercussions. I was wrong again.

This program was the hardest thing I ever dealt with. They made us drug screen randomly, by using colors for the person on certain days at certain times no matter what you were doing or even if you had a ride to get there during their set times. We had to attend classes at least once every day of the week, sometimes more often than that. Then we had to admit that we are addicts aloud to everyone there. And keep in mind I was no longer a social, giving or sharing individual. I did not want anyone to help me other than God, because then I would have had to admit to myself just what I had become!

To top it off, in Drug Court, if you failed to meet any of the requirements, you go back to jail and face the original sentencing for your charges. Especially if the judge thought you were full of crap. I was facing up to fifteen years so there was no way I wasn't going to comply, not until I got through with the program anyway. Then I could go back to my old life and wait for God to take away my addiction. Was this not a messed up way of thinking, rationalizing my thoughts?

After a year, though, sharing my life with others, the program started working. The hardest of all was dealing with the withdrawals from my drugs. I had to pray several times a day for God to give me the strength to make it through a day without using any more drugs. From somewhere the strength came daily, though, and sometimes by the minute!

I made it through the program and at the end of the two years, although I was still an addict, my charges were dismissed. I was no longer a using, practising addict. I no longer had to have my drug of choice every day. It felt good to see things clearly. I made it!

Thinking about all of the events leading up to today in my life, I realize God did answer my prayers. He did take my addiction and gave me back my life.

I live every day knowing that he put me where I needed to be, where I was held accountable for my actions and had to deal with the issues that were overwhelming me.

My God did answer; he took the needle out of my arm. Maybe not the way I had expected, but he did answer in His own way. I am a stronger person, because with His help and the help of others that He put into my path, I no longer have to use any drugs to cope with my everyday life!

I know that my God supplies you with the answer and it's up to you to make the choice, whether to accept His lifelines and use them or to just let them pass you by.

"If a mistake is not a stepping stone, it is a mistake."

~Eli Siegel

Loose Gravel

Blake O'Shea

When Chrissy and I chose the month of August to get married, I wasn't expecting to be serving as a campus minister, heavily involved in getting students settled into the ministry's Christian housing and starting up other activities as the school year began. Celebrating our anniversary each year has been a challenge, too, although somehow we always managed to spend some special time together.

The addition of our daughter, Lily, to our family three years ago, gave us something more to celebrate. Like all children, though, for us, Lily added another step to solving the equation of how to find time for the two of us.

One thing we had enjoyed doing in our 'early days' was riding along the country roads on my motorcycle. So on that Tuesday morning, we decided to drop Lily off at pre-school, get on the bike, and take a little ride. We had three hours before we would need to pick Lily up, so we just took off.

Less than thirty minutes into our ride, we turned onto a county road that had been repaired just a day or two before. For whatever reason, there was a pile of loose gravel that had been used to make the repairs in the road. And although I was only traveling at about 20 mph, when I unknowingly hit that pile of gravel, the bike jerked and before I could correct the situation, we were going down. Even though it happened in a matter of seconds, I felt as if I was in a slow-motion scene of a movie.

My first instinct was to prevent Chrissy from getting hurt. Not having more than a second or two to do something, I hit the throttle, so that she'd fall backwards off the bike instead of being tangled up in it when it fell. My split-second decision worked and the bike landed on me. But in the next split-second, I knew something else had happened; I couldn't feel anything from the neck down.

Thankfully there was a group of houses nearby and it was only a matter of minutes before someone called for help. But those minutes seemed like an eternity. I just remember telling Chrissy over and over how much I loved her. I couldn't see her to know how badly she was hurt, and I definitely couldn't move myself so that I could look at her.

On our way to the local hospital, EMTs kept asking me if I felt 'this'. I didn't. But the logic side of my brain said that would only stand to reason since I'd just had a motorcycle on top of me. I was more concerned they weren't telling me anything about the extent of Chrissy's injuries. It didn't occur to me that the reason they weren't saying much was because of the severity of mine. As it turned out, Chrissy had suffered a severe concussion, and had a few minor scrapes and bruises, but there was nothing life-threatening and nothing that would require continued treatment. It's funny, though, how mothering instinct trumps concussion, and she had the presence of mind about her to make arrangements for Lily to be taken care of.

The following four or five days are forever gone from my memory, but that doesn't mean nothing happened. It didn't take long before it was obvious that I would require more care than the local hospital was capable of providing, so I was transported to a larger facility a couple of hours away that had a spinal injury unit.

Tests showed my spinal cord wasn't severed, but my neck was broken between the 4th and 5th vertebrae and the spinal cord was pinched. Surgery to fuse the broken vertebrae was successful, but time was the only thing that could possibly bring back feeling and use of my arms and legs.

As if being paralyzed wasn't enough, there were other problems to deal with. Among the multiple side effects of injuries such as mine are respiratory problems. Pneumonia, blood clots in my lungs, and a collapsed lung – I had them all, so I was put on a ventilator when it became too difficult for me to breathe on my own.

I was still under a lot of sedation, but I was coherent enough to understand I couldn't move, breathe, or talk. Was this going to be my life indefinitely? If so, I didn't want to live.

I could hear, though. I heard the doctors telling Chrissy and my mom that the longer someone is on a ventilator, the harder it is to come off one. Thankfully, I also heard that the doctors were going to be aggressive in their plan to get me breathing on my own as soon as possible.

When I did come off the ventilator, though, breathing without help was still too difficult and a tracheotomy tube was inserted. That, along with a heightened awareness of my surroundings and situation, started making everything I'd been through very painfully real.

I was paralyzed. There is no way anyone can possibly understand the sea of emotions unless they're, well, someone who's been in my position. Uselessness, hope, fear, self-pity, anger, thankfulness to be alive, wishing you weren't (alive, that is), joy in even the tiniest of improvements, imagining improvements out of sheer desperation...it's all there in no particular order or at any given time. There were even times when the practical side of my personality would take over and I'd fret over the details of what was supposed to be taking place at work; things I needed to be doing.

Student activities still needed to go on – activities I was in charge of; the ministry's housing facility for male college students was full (half of them incoming freshmen students) and all the things other that went with being a campus minister.

I was blessed to have a secretary, who is like an older sister to me. She had both the ability and the heart to jump in with both feet to keep the ministry and the house running. She stepped up and did an amazing job; dealing with everything like a pro. She, along with a wonderfully supportive board of directors, went so far above and beyond the call of duty – there are no words to sufficiently describe how grateful I am for all they've done. Their actions made it possible for me to focus on therapy, learning also to adjust to my new state of being, to how it was affecting Chrissy and Lily, and to prepare myself for the possibility of never getting any better.

Two weeks or so after the tracheotomy, they removed the tube. Finally! I was able to breathe on my own and talk!

What a relief it was to speak. It was the one and only aspect of my life that was unchanged by the accident.

Unfortunately, therapy did little more than keep me from having complete atrophy in my muscles. After a pre-designated period of time, both the therapy center and our health insurance company said it was futile to continue the rigorous pace. I would be this way for the rest of my life.

Four years later, I'm still unable to feel anything below my shoulders. I can lift my arms; even swing them from side to side a bit. By putting a pencil in my hand brace, I can peck away on the keyboard of my laptop and punch in phone numbers on the telephone. Hey, I may be slow, but I eventually get the job done.

By the grace of God, a supportive board of directors and a secretary turned ministry administrator, I've been able to minister to the students on the university in a limited, but meaningful way.

Is it my desire to walk again; to hug my wife and daughter close, to throw a Frisbee, mow my lawn, brush my teeth, feed myself…? You bet it is! In the weeks and months following the accident, the focus on people's comments was that they were praying for a miracle; that I'd walk again…and soon! That was my prayer, as well. But as time went on, I began to realize that the true miracle I've been given is life. The other health issues that come with paralysis, and the fact that I am able to persevere through them...that is my miracle, and I'm thankful for it each and every day of my life.

"I have sometimes been wildly, despairingly, acutely miserable, but through it all I still know quite certainly that just to be alive is a grand thing."

~Agatha Christie

Late for Dance Class

Cassy Fox

I was part of my high school 'ag' team for livestock judging and we'd made arrangements with a local horse stable so we could go out after school to practice judging the horses for an upcoming competition. Because I was the youngest on the team and didn't yet have a driver's license, I was going to ride with the student teacher who was heading up the team as part of her training. And because the farm we were going to was fairly close to my family's farm, she said she'd just drop me off at home when we were done. Sounded like a good plan, right? And it was, but we all know things don't always go as planned….

We were done at the stable and the rest of the kids were getting ready to leave. My teacher, however, decided she was going to stay a while longer. I reminded her that she'd promised to give me a ride home, and that I needed to leave so that I'd not be late for dance class that evening. I know, dance and agriculture don't sound like they go together, but dancing is my passion. Agriculture is something I know and did because it came easy for me.

Although our teacher was really sweet, she was still a college student and not experienced in making sound decisions in this sort of situation. Her reply was for me to catch a ride with one of the other kids.

Well, this might not have been the end of the world, but the guys on the team weren't the type of guys I'd consider getting in a car with. Besides, even if I would have, my parents would have grounded me for life as soon as they found out.

My only other option was Sara, who was a good friend. Our parents were friends, too. The only problem was that Sarah had only had her license for a few months and her parents had the same rule as mine; no passengers for the first year or until given permission to do so. But she knew why I didn't want to go with the guys and she wasn't going to leave me. So she spoke up and offered me a ride home. I had to get home, after all. My mom was at the dentist with my little sister and my dad and older siblings were at work. We were less than five miles from home. What could it hurt?

When Sara and I got in the car, she considered calling her mom, but in the end decided asking forgiveness would be easier than getting permission, so off we went. Sara was a careful driver and we were doing fine until she almost missed the turn off the highway onto the county road I lived on. She'd been to my house lots of times, but had always come from the other direction. Coming from this direction, the road did kind of sneak up on you, and was in the middle of a hill, so it was easy to do.

Had Sara been an experienced driver, she would have gone on, turned around at the next road and come back. But she panicked and instead, tried to make the turn. Making a full left turn doing fifty isn't something I'd recommend. She made the turn, but lost control and hit a utility pole head-on my side, causing the pole to snap, bringing the power lines down with it. Glass shattered and the force of the impact caused the air-bags to inflate. The car was smashed accordion-style; making it impossible for the doors to be opened. What remained of the utility pole was literally less than a foot from my face.

Seeing the blood streaming down each other's arms and face sent us both into sheer panic. We were screaming and crying as the sparks from the power lines against the metal of the car were popping and cracking. Were we going to die?

Sara kept asking me if I was alright. She was crying and begging me not to die. Hearing her saying the word die over and over only fueled the frenzy. All I could think about was that I wanted my mom. I started pulling my phone out of my pocket to call her.

My mom's my best friend, and all I could think about was being in her arms. I was shaking so badly I don't know how I punched the number in, but I did. When she answered I couldn't stop crying and screaming, "Mommy we crashed! We crashed and there's blood and glass and I want you, Mommy!"

I can't even begin to imagine how she held it together, but she did. Her voice was shaky, but somehow she managed to calm me down enough for me to tell her where I was, who I was with, that we were both hurt, that the power lines were on the car, and that Sara was calling 911. My mom said she was on her way.

As well as being a farmer, my dad is a state patrolman, and was on duty when 911 got the call. He heard it over the radio in his patrol car, and, because of the location, immediately started in our direction. Mom was trying to call him as he was responding to his call, but when they connected, he told her he was almost there, he'd let her know as soon as he knew something.

With over twenty years of service at the time, he'd worked accident scenes even the most graphic of movies wouldn't touch, but this was different. This one involved his daughter.

It was only minutes before dad, along with several other state patrolmen and the ambulance arrived. Both Mom and Sara's mom and dad arrived shortly after that. The EMTs worked as quickly as possible to get us out of the car after the power lines were no longer a safety issue. They put us on stretches and moved us to the grassy area on the side of the road to assess our condition. We were fortunate.

Neither of us sustained any serious injuries. Our arms and faces were cut up pretty badly and we had glass embedded in our arms and face, we had bruising from the force of the airbags against our chests. Sara's foot was badly sprained from getting twisted under the accelerator and my back and neck were sprained from being whipped up and back so hard when we hit the pole. After a more extensive examination at the hospital, we were both released and able to go home that evening.

While we were at the hospital, we were finally able to relate the entire chain of events to our parents. After hearing what had taken place and the circumstances surrounding the wreck, they all agreed we'd done the right thing and weren't angry with us. They even went so far as to say that under the circumstances, they probably wouldn't have done anything different. Well, nothing but trying to turn when you'd almost missed the road. They were, however, angry with the student teacher for her lack of maturity.

Physical recovery didn't take long. Within a couple of weeks we were both pretty much back to normal. But emotional recovery was a lot longer in coming. Sara was afraid to drive. I didn't want to ride in the car or even go down our road on the school bus. I couldn't without going past the accident scene. But I couldn't hide out forever, so I would lie down in the seat until we were past it. And it was literally years before I would, under any circumstances, be in a vehicle that was going to take that left turn onto our road.

Sara and I graduated from high school and went our separate ways. She married locally and still lives in our home town. I left to pursue a career in astrophysics and marry the man of my dreams. But there will always be a connection between us. We endured one of the most frightening events of our lives together, and that's something you just don't forget. I'll always have a place in my heart for her...even though she did make me miss my dance class.

"There is only one thing more painful than learning from experience, and that is not learning from experience." ~Laurence J. Peter

Don't Open the Door

Marlene Andreasen

Life was good...not great! I'd graduated from high school just weeks earlier, was engaged to my high school sweetheart, and planning my dream wedding. And as if that wasn't enough, I had a job I loved. No, make that two jobs I loved. I'd been working at a local bank all year as part of my business program at school. When I graduated, they promoted me to a position I enjoyed and told me I was exactly what they were looking for in terms of short and long-range employee advancement. But I'd been working in a department store at the mall since I was sixteen and loved it so much that I continued to work there a few hours a week, too.

That's where I'd been-working – at the mall – the evening not opening the door probably saved my life.

It was around nine-thirty. I was still living at home, but my family had gone to my brother's ball game for the evening, so after changing into my PJ's, I sat down to finish placing the order for our wedding invitations. I'd just finished and was picking up the phone to call my fiancé when someone started ringing the doorbell...over and over and over again.

It startled me, to say the least. When had anyone ever rung our doorbell at ten o'clock at night?

My first inclination told me it was my younger brother – being a younger brother, and most likely excited over a win. I was just about ready to swing the door open to congratulate him, when I felt strangely cold all over. Something told me to look out the mini panes in the door – that opening it would not be good.

Instead of my family, I saw a sloppily dressed man. He was trying to look in to see if I was there while pointing up at the sky excitedly. His hand was on the door knob. I started shaking all over. Wondering where he came from, I looked past him and saw a beat-up old station wagon parked in front of the neighbor's house.

The man saw me look out the window, and then walk away. He started ringing the doorbell again, and again. I tried to ignore it but by this time I was crying and shaking so hard. I just prayed he'd go away. After a little while he stopped ringing the bell. Did I dare look to see if he'd driven away? I carefully lifted the curtain in the dining room. His car was still there. Where was he?

I turned to go back into the kitchen to call my fiancé, but just as I did, I saw the man looking in the window of the kitchen door that opened onto the deck. I stifled a scream and grabbed the phone. But as I did, he started pulling on the door knob and shaking it. I was terrified!

This was before 911, so I somehow dialed the number for the police that was on the handle of the phone. In between sobs I told them what was happening, gave them my address and hung up. Next, I ran to the other exterior door of the house to make sure it was secure and then ran back to the phone to call my fiancé.

As I was telling him what was happening, I saw the man walk back past the kitchen window, looking in to see where I was. I ducked down, and then put the phone down long enough to see him get into his car and drive away. I tried to get his licence number, but the plate was missing.

A couple of minutes later the police got there-about the time my parents got home. I was able to give a fairly detailed description of both the man and the car, but the police could really do nothing more than drive around looking for him to question him.

I understandably didn't sleep well that night, and the next day, I couldn't concentrate on anything. I kept hoping the police would call saying they'd found him. They called, alright. But I wasn't prepared for what they had to say.

About an hour after the man left our house, he broke into the apartment of a single girl in her twenties. He beat her viciously with a baseball bat and raped her.

The police saw him getting back into his car after the attack and took him in for questioning. By the time they got to the police station with him, the girl had called the police to report the attack. She told the dispatcher she'd been able to hit him in the head with a lamp from her nightstand and as a result he was bleeding from the forehead. The man the police had in custody had a nasty gash in his forehead.

Because the girl who'd been raped could, and did, identify him, they said it wasn't necessary that I do so, but I did any way. I needed to see the whole incident through to the end. He was later convicted for several crimes against the other girl and sent to prison.

Life went on, and it's been a great one, but to this day, I still don't open the door unless I'm sure. Very sure.

"Turn your wounds into wisdom." ~Oprah Winfrey

Hurricane Honeymoon

Mara Suranno

Jason and I got married the same weekend we graduated from college. Money was tight and we both had jobs we were starting right away, so we didn't have the resources or the time for a real honeymoon. Instead, we settled for a couple of nights on the road to where we'd be living.

We didn't mind, but made a commitment to celebrate our fifth anniversary with a nice long vacation— a honeymoon to somewhere tropical.

A few months before our fifth anniversary, Jason reminded me of the trip we'd planned (as if I needed reminding). We discussed our options and decided on Cozumel. The price would allow us to stay longer than we could if we chose somewhere more 'exotic' and since we're not what you could consider well-traveled, we liked the 'all inclusive' aspects of the package. We booked the trip and started counting the days.

As the time of our departure got closer, we started getting wind of tropical storms heading that way (no pun intended). We joked that it would be just our luck, but didn't really think it would hamper our much-anticipated get-away. Wrong!

The plane landed and we were taxied to our resort under sunny skies and balmy breezes; just what we'd hoped for. But by the next morning, the winds had picked up to the point of making it impossible to enjoy the beach. By lunch time, the staff were posting emergency procedures throughout the resort and announcing over the intercom that the tropical storm we'd seen on the weather before we'd left home was now hurricane Wilma, a category four, expected to hit the area in the early morning hours. They said it was essential that all guests follow the posted emergency procedures to the letter.

Like I said, we weren't well traveled and this certainly wasn't the experience we were hoping for. But it was too late to turn back now. We had no choice but to ride it out and hope and pray for the best.

I don't think anyone really slept much that night. The restaurants were unusually quiet, even though there were plenty of people eating. Everyone was more interested in listening to the weather updates (translated to English), and the news wasn't good.

In the early morning hours, just as predicted, the storm hit. We lost power almost immediately and everyone was ordered to go to the dining rooms.

When we arrived, everyone was given a key-type mechanism to get in and out of their rooms (the key cards were electronic and would no longer work), but we were told we wouldn't be allowed to come and go at will. We were told we would be issued bottles of water and that every effort was being made to keep everyone safe.

As the storm raged on, the roof and two top levels of the resort were blown away, the winds blew out windows and uprooted trees. Debris was everywhere.

Meanwhile, Jason and I clung to one another – trying our best to keep our wits about us and to stay focused on what the staff was doing. We figured, if we watched them closely enough, we'd be ready for whatever came next. But I don't think two rural Mid-Westerners like Jason and I could have ever been ready for what took place.

We were allowed to return to our rooms to gather our things, we were urged to bring any valuables and a couple of changes of clothing with us back to the dining facilities. Once we returned, everyone was given fresh fruit and soft drinks.

The manager of the resort began to give a report on the state of things and explained what would be taking place.

Due to the lack of power, everyone had to stay in a central location. The generator power – which was limited – would be reserved for operation of bathroom facilities. Breaks would be limited, though, to three per day, and we were told not to ask to use the restroom at other times unless absolutely necessary.

Then we were told about the looters; that their arrival was a near certainty but that the Mexican police were doing everything they could to protect those visiting the country. If at all possible, guards would be supplied.

Looters! Were we in danger? It never occurred to me that we had something other than the storm to fear.

When the looters did come, though, they did little more than raid the supply of food and water. Jason, being the loving protector that he is, had me sit with my back up against the wall and he sat in front of me; leaning back on me in an effort to shield me from view. The fact that they didn't speak English was frightening since we didn't know what they were saying, but thankfully their interaction with the guests was minimal and without incident.

For the next four days, Jason and I lived in the darkened dining room of the resort with about a hundred and sixty other people, most of them Americans. What water the looters hadn't taken was limited; one bottle for every two people per day. Food was limited to crackers, nuts, oranges, bananas, and other fruit that didn't spoil.

The bathroom breaks were the worst. Their generator power wasn't enough to allow for flushing so staff members would flush after every ten uses or so.

While some people were cautiously friendly, others were obviously in a 'survival of the fittest' mode. It was frightening to see people's self-seeking, animalistic attitudes. It was hard enough not knowing when we'd get to leave and worrying about what our family and friends back home were going through not knowing we were alive. Having to worry about your fellow 'captives' turning on you was something we shouldn't have had to deal with.

But we didn't dare sleep. People were stealing water bottles that had even the smallest amounts left. Fights broke out over space, food, bathroom lines…you name it. Others were bribing staff members with money and jewelry to get extra food and water. It was horrible!

The Mexican government and emergency reaction teams aren't as advanced as their American equivalents, so progress in repairs and assistance was slow. But after six days, we were told we could leave and that the airlines were honoring tickets; beginning with flights that were scheduled to have left on the 15th and so on. One more day!!

One week and one day after we'd arrived, we left Mexico and headed for home. Home sweet home.

While I am proud of the way Jason and I handled ourselves in such adverse situations, it's not something I'd care to repeat. But it's not the storm that bothers me. What bothered me most was seeing people turn on one another instead of coming together to make a bad situation a little bit better for everyone. I hope and pray I never feel that my needs are more important than those of everyone else in the same situation I am in.

> *"If you have integrity, nothing else matters. If you don't have integrity, nothing else matters."*
> *~Alan Simpson*

Will I Ever Know the Joys of Being a Mother

Linette Boisvert

I asked myself and God every day if I'd ever know what it felt like to be a mother; to feel a child's arms around my neck, to read a bedtime story, to see the joy and wonder in a little one's eyes on Christmas morning....

When Sean and I started dating, I paid particular attention to how he reacted to my older brother's kids. I'd always loved kids. Not to brag, but I was the babysitter of choice for all the kids in the neighborhood and at our church. In fact, I earned enough money babysitting that I never had any other type of part-time job growing up. I bought a car and was able to have other things teenage girls consider essential. I even saved enough to help with college expenses.

Whoever I married had to love kids and Sean clearly did. When it was obvious things were getting serious between us, we discussed the issue and were both looking forward to being parents. When we were married a little more than a year later, we decided not to wait too long to start a family.

Then, when another year had passed and I still wasn't pregnant, I started worrying and stressing over the fact to the point of near-obsession. We both made appointments for physicals and to make sure everything was working as it should, so to speak. The doctors discovered, however, that I had luteal phase defect, which meant I didn't produce enough progesterone for my uterus to house a fertilized egg.

The fact that luteal phase defect is usually treatable was encouraging, though, so we started treatments, monitoring my temperature and all the things we thought might help. Two years later, we still didn't have a baby.

Sean and I were fortunate that our relationship was strong enough to weather the pain and frustration of infertility. It still took a toll on my self-esteem and our hearts were heavy with desire. At that point, we decided to pursue adoption. We had too much love to give to spend the rest of our lives trying to make the impossible happen. We devoted our energies to home studies, applications, and case studies.

We were elated, only three months after being approved, when a young, unwed mother selected us to be the mother of her soon-to-be born baby.

The adoption was to be a semi-open one; we would meet the mother, be present for the birth and send quarterly updates on the baby's progress. But, without our written consent, she would not be able to visit or contact us.

The day of our son's birth was the happiest I'd ever known. But that happiness turned to terror the very next day. When we arrived at the hospital to fill out the birth certificate and take our son home, mother and baby were gone! She'd left a note for the nurse to give us saying she was sorry, but that she just couldn't go through with it.

That was it. A simple "I'm sorry". We had an agreement – a contract – but none of that mattered. As the birth mother she had the right to change her mind. There was nothing to do but accept the facts and go forward…without a child.

Devastation doesn't even begin to express what we were feeling. We were raw and weren't sure we'd ever be able to trust anyone again. Our adoption counselor advised us to take a few days and get away by ourselves to try to process our thoughts and emotions. But, she said, she refused to let us give up on being parents. "You two have too much love and too much heart to give up. I think the child you're meant to have just isn't here yet."

While her kind words were appreciated, we weren't prepared to hear them at that point. It was hard for us to believe we ever would be parents after what we had been through.

Four months later, though, just after Thanksgiving, our case worker called to ask if we would be willing to consider adopting not one, but two children; a two year old boy and his sibling (sex unknown) that was due in a matter of weeks. Their mother, who'd made one poor choice after another, was willing to surrender her parental rights for a boyfriend who didn't want to be tied down.

My heart was pounding in my head and my stomach was in knots. Were we? Could we risk this again? I was afraid to speak for fear I'd let my heart win out over my head without talking to Sean. So taking a deep breath, I told her I'd talk to Sean and get back to her by the end of the day.

The next couple of weeks were agonizing. What if she changed her mind? What if the grandparents decided they wanted them after all?

We were making the hour-long drive to my parents' house on Christmas Eve when Sean's phone rang. Could we possibly pick up our sons at the hospital the next afternoon, the case worker wanted to know?

Six years later, being a mother is still everything I hoped it would be and more! Harry and Gage bring more joy to our lives each and every day, but on Christmas Eve, the day we celebrate both their birthdays, we're especially thankful.

"Each day comes bearing its own gifts.

Untie the ribbons."

~Ruth Ann Schabacker

I'll be Seeing You

Misty Mills

I was always a sap for old movies. Nostalgia was my 'middle name' and I even decorated our apartment in 1940s styled furnishings and fabrics. One part of this era I had no desire to relive, though, was characterized by the grief and pain hundreds of thousands of wives, mothers, and girlfriends had to experience when their loved ones were injured, killed, or missing as a result of World War II.

But since I'd married my high school sweetheart, who 'just happened' to be a marine, I knew that there was always a possibility I would know what it was to lose my husband to war.

On 9-11, what had been a remote possibility suddenly became less than remote. A few months after that tragedy, Bryce received his orders to go to Iraq.

"It'll be okay," he promised. "I'll be back before you know it. And they have a computer lab in the compound with SKYPE. We'll at least be able to see each other."

That was some consolation, but not enough to make the sick feeling in my stomach go away. I just couldn't imagine life without Bryce. Without Bryce, I wouldn't have a life.

We chose not to attend the farewell gala. Instead, we stayed at home, ate pizza by candle light, and danced to our favorite songs – mine being "I'll Be Seeing You." (I told you I was a sap for nostalgia.)

I didn't think my heart would ever ache as badly as it did the day we'd said goodbye, when he left for boot camp five years earlier. I was wrong, though. His departure for Iraq was worse, and the next several days, when we couldn't contact each other, were grueling. I consoled myself with the fact that he wasn't even in Iraq yet, so at least he wasn't in harm's way.

When his unit finally did arrive, they were all given a brief amount of time to SKYPE with someone before going through their 'initiation' of sorts to life in the desert. And Bryce had never looked so good.

Things went as well as they could for the next few months. I was terribly lonely and lived for our twice a week SKYPE dates. Living on base did give me the advantage of having other wives around who understood what I was going through. And while there are those who use their husband's absence as an excuse for being unfaithful and set a less-than-stellar example, there are plenty of us who are faithful, loving, supportive wives, leaning on each other for moral support.

Another advantage to living on base is not having to depend on the news to know what's going on. There are daily bulletins posted on the Corps website on each unit. And while the news wasn't always what we wanted to hear, at least it was real and not exaggerated.

Four months into their deployment, I sat down to the computer for our SKYPE date. But Bryce didn't call. I swallowed a lump in my throat, but didn't panic. Hey, he was in a war zone. We'd been blessed to have had things as good as they'd been. I didn't sleep much that night, but was sure I'd hear from him the next day.

"Misty, do you need me to come over?" My friend, Janelle, asked when I answered my phone.

"Why," I asked. "What's wrong?"

"I'm on my way. Check the bulletins."

Shaking, I typed in the web address. Bryce's unit had come under fire; three casualties, two MIA and multiple wounded. No, I thought. I'd know if it was Bryce. Surely I'd know by now.

Janelle arrived just moments before the MP's. They regretted to inform me that my husband, Sergeant Bryce

Mills was reported missing in action in the…. I couldn't breathe. I couldn't see straight. I heard their voices but couldn't respond.

The next few days were filled with friends dropping by, sitting with me until I fell asleep, and trying to cheer me up. After three or four weeks, they started encouraging me to get back into a normal routine. But my life wasn't normal. Bryce was gone and no one could tell me when, or if, he was ever coming back. I became lethargic and depressed.

My parents came to take me 'home' with them for a while, thinking the change of scenery would do me good. They tried so hard to make things better. But the more they tried, the deeper I sank into depression. I even contemplated taking my life. After all, if Bryce wasn't in my life, I didn't really have one.

I'll never forget the night I lay there in my old bedroom at my parents' house thinking about what it would be like to be dead – to not feel the pain of missing Bryce any more. I knew what it would do to my parents, but at that point I couldn't even bring myself to care enough to not make them feel what I was feeling. The decision was made. Then my parents left the next morning for their usual Saturday trip to the nursing home to visit my great aunt.

Feeling almost relieved, I lay back on the pillow, put my ear buds in, and picked up my Ipod. I absent-mindedly ran through the songs, but before I could select something, my IPod did it for me. The song; "I'll be Seeing You." But if I hadn't known it was impossible, I would have sworn it was Bryce singing it. Why this song? Was this his way of telling me he was waiting for me? Or was it something else?

"Oh, Bryce, I miss you," I sobbed. "I want to see you, too."

"Misty, Misty!" My dad was pounding on the door. "Misty, you need to come downstairs right away!"

My dad wasn't the type to get excited over nothing, so, drying my eyes and taking a deep breath, I got up and opened the door. Dad, after giving me a little hug, took me by the arm and led me toward the stairs.

On the fourth step, you can see into the living room and what I saw was my precious Bryce! He was using canes and had a jagged scar across his forehead, but he was really there! Alive! In my parents' living room!

I couldn't quit crying – sobbing is more like it. We held on to each other for dear life and wouldn't let go. My parents were crying as much as we were, I think.

When his unit had been ambushed, he and the other guy that had been reported missing had hid out in a cave for several days. Their wounds made it impossible for them to try making it back to safety on their own, so they decided to take turns watching for friendly transport back.

Before that could happen, they were taken prisoner by a random group of radicals who looked at their captives like trophies in a case. They fed them, but had no way to provide much-needed medical care. Their group also lacked any real leadership and organization, so they spent more time arguing among themselves than they did tormenting Bryce and Larry. In fact, it was their arguing that drew the attention of our troops, who consequently found Bryce and Larry.

Bryce said he'd insisted on not contacting me; that he wanted to do it himself. He said he couldn't bear the thought of someone else seeing my face when I learned he was coming home to me.

Bryce eventually made a full recovery and we're still in the Marines, where Bryce serves as a drill instructor. I'll never forget the ordeal of his being missing, but even more than that, I'll never forget the lesson I learned in never losing hope. I know it just as easily could have turned out differently. Knowing what he and so many others go through for our freedom, and knowing what they experience when they come back home to the ones they love. I now know that we owe it to each and every one of them to live life to the fullest and enjoy the freedoms we have for as long as we can.

"Hope is faith holding out its hand in the dark."
~George Iles

First Love, Second Chance

Francine Jacobs

Joey was my high school sweetheart. He was everything any girl would want in a boyfriend – thoughtful, funny, romantic and not the 'if you love me you'll have sex' kind of guy. We enjoyed a lot of the same things, my family liked him as much as I did, we had a great group of friends...life was good. We were crazy in love with one another. The 'problem' was that Joey was a year younger than me. That meant I'd be leaving him behind to go to college. Another issue was that I really didn't know what I wanted to do. I'd thought about being a nurse for years. There was an excellent nursing program at the university in our home town. I could do that and not leave Joey. That sounded good, and it was definitely what he wanted me to do, but I was feeling the tug of going to the same Christian college my aunts and uncles had all gone to. There was no nursing program, but they'd all gone there....

Joey never pressured me about anything until I started leaning toward going away to school. And even then it wasn't pressure, but more imploring. "Please," he said. "Just stay one year and give the university a try. If you don't like it we can leave together next year."

I'm still not sure why, but I left. Biggest mistake of my life. Joey was hurt and I missed him terribly. We managed to keep things going that first semester. Then school started getting really hard for me. I'd never been the top of the class kind of student so it took all I had to keep up. Maybe it was because my heart wasn't completely in my classes, but by Spring break, I was more miserable than ever and Joey and I decided our relationship was over.

I spent the next three years struggling through classes. I was attracted to some of the guys, but I think I was so desperate to fill the empty spot left from Joey, I just tried too hard. I was always the girl friend not the girlfriend.

I graduated, worked for a year, and then enrolled in the local technical college's LPN program. I loved it! I felt like I was finding my niche, but that made me feel guiltier than ever about Joey and me. I still thought about him all the time, but he'd married the previous year. And me, well, I was still trying too hard to find that someone special in my life.

I met Dave through a mutual friend. He was different from Joey in a lot of ways, but we had a good time together.

He was lonely, too; his wife had abandoned him and their two children three years earlier.

A few months later when Dave and I announced we were getting married, my family was less than thrilled. My dad and sister actually begged me not to marry him. I should have listened.

The first year was great. Dave and I even talked about having a child of our own. I started to worry, though, when after a year, I didn't get pregnant. But he was reassuring and we kept trying. After another year, though, he started insinuating that it was my fault because there was "obviously nothing wrong with him."

Shortly thereafter, the physical abuse started. I put up with it because I was: a) embarrassed to admit I'd made such a mistake; b) thought it too late to ever have anyone else to spend my life with; and c) thought I could get him to change.

But the day I was helping our office manager redo the filing system was the day I discovered what a lie my entire marriage had been. I looked in Dave's file and found out that after he and his first wife had had Carissa, he'd had a vasectomy! All the tears I shed and guilt I felt for not being able to conceive – and he'd known all along the reason why!

I'd spent all these years living a lie! I was devastated and scared. The hatred I felt for him in that moment was frightening to me. I didn't know I was capable of feeling something so intensely that was so bad. If he'd lied about that, what else had he lied about?

Plenty, it turns out. I still can't believe I was able to act so normal while I went around gathering information. I was formulating a plan to confront him with everything and then end the marriage immediately. Nothing was going to change my mind. I took precautions to protect myself from him when I told him by having my best friend waiting outside without his knowledge. He got angry, alright, but thankfully took his anger out on the furniture and the bedroom wall instead of me. I left with no intention of ever looking back.

Two weeks later, though, Dave walked into the doctor's office with a gun. What had I done? I was putting innocent lives at risk! I was as mortified as I was scared. Guilt was in no short supply, either. Thankfully no one was hurt; Dave was taken to a facility for evaluation and was admitted for treatment. While he was there, I packed everything I could, called my family and moved back to my home town; several hundred miles from the pain and embarrassment. I needed a new start.

I'd been back for a couple of months, when my doorbell rang. Standing on the other side of the door when I opened it was Joey. "Hey, remember me," he smiled. Wow, that smile...it still melted my heart.

We talked well into the night. He told me he'd married the girl he dated after me, that they had a daughter, but that the marriage ended a few short years later. The 'official' cause for the divorce was her affair and desire to marry the other man. But, he said, "I'm as much to blame as she was; I never could really give her my heart because you still had it."

Joey and I started seeing one another and it wasn't long before we knew what we had known all those years ago, but that I was too blind and immature to admit – that we had belonged together for ever.

Five months later Joey and I were married with our families and closest friends there to celebrate with us. Joey was my first love and my forever love. I'm just thankful for second chances.

"Absence diminishes small loves and increases great ones, as the wind blows out the candle and fans the bonfire."

~François Duc de La Rochefoucauld

Sometimes All We Need is a Friend

Project Hope – Remembering the Past, Looking to the Future

Russell Johnson

In the early hours of August 6, 2007, our neighboring Emery County experienced seismic activity that set off a chain of events that have culminated in a great tragedy and tremendous sorrow. Nine lives were lost in what has been called the Crandall Canyon mine disaster. Six lives were lost from the initial mine collapse and sadly three more lives were lost in a rescue attempt. You can imagine how this devastating event would have an impact on this community. Now, about six weeks later, it was time to help contribute to the healing process.

"Project Hope" was launched through four business classes that I teach at a small community college in Southern Utah. Each semester I try to implement an element of "service learning" in each class. A sense of contributing and giving back to society is very important for a well-rounded individual and is, at times, difficult to teach or to experience. Somewhere, somehow, someone suggested we provide a barbecue for the whole town of Huntington where most of the victims were from. So "Project Hope" was born. The idea was to spread a little hope and cheer in their time of sadness and need. We wanted these people to know that we were thinking of them as they try and get their lives back together. We would feed the whole town and give away 1200 tribute t-shirts with the names of those lives lost on the back. So that's what we did...

Teams were organized and assignments were made. This is no small task. Six newspapers promoted and reported on our event. We raised money. A lot of money for a small community. How could you turn down a letter signed by so many students and for such a great cause? Corporate sponsors, businesses large and small, and Snow College faculty, staff, and students contributed to this event.

The day of the event arrived. We donned our own T-shirts, loaded vehicles with supplies, and off we went. We towed a large barbecue on wheels behind one of the trucks. We loaded up a golf-cart to make rounds in the city to remind residents of the free meal later that day. We began to cook 300 pounds of Sanpete marinated turkey barbecue. You've never tasted turkey like this before.

The Salt Lake Tribune started their story by saying, "Still reeling quite a bit from the prolonged trauma of the Crandall Canyon mine disaster, the folks of Huntington received a little tender loving care this week from some Snow College students. About 80 business students from Snow College in Ephraim, on the other side of the mountain threw a free barbecue for the whole town Thursday." Hundreds gathered for this kind gesture under the large shade trees at the Huntington City Park. 1200 T-shirts were given away that said, "Remembering the past, looking to the future," with the names of those whose lives were lost, on the back. The Tribune ended the article with this: "It's very special," said Kay Truman, his gray hair poking out from under a cowboy hat, "for young people to have that much feeling for a town they're not familiar with...in my life, I've never seen people from other places go to this extent."

Mayor Hilary Gordon was touched by the outpouring as well. "One takes food to one's neighbor when somebody dies or is sick," she said, "I never would have thought of feeding a whole community. It's just an awesome tribute, unique."

Kascee, a student, said, "A woman came up to me who was almost in tears…she expressed her gratitude three or four times during our short conversation…I had many others who shook my hand or even embraced me with a hug. I know they were very appreciative."

Jonathan, another student, said, "Helping with the barbecue in Huntington has been a highlight of my Snow College experience. I was able to go door to door to announce the barbecue, and to hear the positive comments from the people. It's awesome to see other people happy!"

Marlon, "I thought the project was awesome! I liked getting the hands on experience. Seeing the different ways to market it, raising money, etc., was good. I had never done anything like that in a college class before. It was way cool."

And finally, Rodney. "As a young Hispanic woman was going through the line, I overheard her talking to her daughter. I then spoke to the young daughter in Spanish and the woman turned to me, and with gratitude in her heart expressed her thanks for the barbecue and told me to tell everyone back at Snow College 'thank you!'"

Here are some comments from community members young and old:

-Thank you so much for this. My Uncle's name is on the back of your shirt. We really appreciate your kindness.

-Can I take a shirt for a little boy of one of the miners? He still thinks his daddy is coming back home.

-Thank you so much for putting on this barbecue. We haven't been able to relax since this tragedy has happened. It has been nice to come out and sit down, eat, and just talk to our neighbors.

-Mommy, why is Snow College doing this? What can we do nice for Snow College?

It was an amazing experience for me and my students. For a moment the bigger picture of life became very clear in our minds. Other things didn't seem to matter as much. My students were visiting with the residents and playing *red rover* with the young children who really didn't quite comprehend what was going on. It was a long, tiring day, but well worth the effort. It felt good. It feels good to do good and give back, even if in just a small way. What a great life lesson for my students and me.

That day, that event, these Snow College students learned a little bit about business and a whole lot about life.

"Remembering the past, looking to the future!"

"It's easy to make a buck. It's a lot tougher to make a difference." ~Tom Brokaw

Meeting Judy

Norman Mitchell

Today is Saturday and we just left my mom's after visiting her at home and having a nice lunch with her. We come out here every other Saturday to visit with her. She has been quite lonely since dad died a few months back in that dreadful car accident.

All of our lives have changed pretty dramatically and each of us died a little that day with dad. As most people would agree, a life ending at the age of fifty-five has ended way too early, especially for an energetic man who had been blessed with good health his whole life. His life ended abruptly, and most days it seems that mom's life has as well.

There is typically a silver lining for each visit and it's one of the best parts about our visits. Each time, when my mom sees my two kids running to her and yelling, "Grandma," she gets a big smile on her face. Typically that is the only time my mom has smiles. This week was a little different though, she definitely seemed more upbeat. After she had given a plate full of cookies to the kids, I asked her my usual question about how she was doing. I was anticipating some tears of sorrow, some expressions of loneliness. I expected to feel some potential guilt on my part for having to leave her yet again. Her answer was different from what I expected, though; it brought joy to my heart.

She told me she was doing better and that each day she has more and more peace. Undoubtedly, I was relieved to hear that her heart was mending and wanted to find out what had happened to point her back to God, point her back to all the people who were still here and loved her very much. At church a few weeks back, she had been introduced to another widow by the name of Judy.

Judy also had lost her husband a couple years ago and she was around mom's age. After a lot of encouragement by Judy, mom finally decided to have lunch with her.

Their one lunch turned into a three hours meeting filled with hugs, tears, scripture and prayers. The next day they got together for lunch again except at Judy's house this time. Their time together at lunch carried over into the dinner hour and mom finally left Judy's house about 10:00 pm. This time was a little different though, there was a lot of study and prayer again, but also there was laughter and discussions that had nothing to do with loss and grief. Mom was starting to heal.

After hearing about what has now become a daily ritual for mom and Judy, I asked when we might be able to meet this fine lady. Low and behold, Judy walked in the door before mom could speak. As I stood up to introduce myself and my family, Judy gave me a big hug before I could say a word. Judy said, "I know who you are – I feel like I know you so well." She then jumped over and gave my wife a big hug, then picked up both my children and asked them to give their Grandma Judy a big hug. When she put them down, she pulled out a couple pieces of candy and slipped them into my kid's hands and whispered to them, "Here is a piece of candy for later," just like any good grandmother would do.

In the past couple weeks, mom had made a friend – a really good friend. After some more hugs and a few tears of joy we all sat down. Mom and Judy told us about their studies and both finding peace with the hand that was dealt to each of them. You see, Judy was still grieving and they both needed each other. We found out a lot about Judy and found out that she and her husband were never able to have children, which is why her loneliness and grieving had lasted so long.

The time had come for us to make the 90 minute trip back home so we started to say our goodbyes. I thanked Judy from the bottom of my heart for being there for mom in way that I was unable to be. Judy, with a tear in her eye and a smile on her face, said to me, "Actually I want to thank you. You have an incredible mother. She has helped me more in the past two weeks than anyone else has been able to for the past two years."

Judy then hugged my wife and kids, and told me we were now her family too. Our kids now have two grandmothers there, both of whom want to spoil them rotten.

We went to visit mom, anticipating depression and tears and we walked away with smiles and peace. Mom is happy and on the mend. She also has a friend – a good friend – who can help carry her sorrows. Most importantly, I feel great joy in my heart knowing she doesn't blame God for dad's death any more. She is facing towards God and looking to Him daily for the strength that only He can give. The biggest blessing is in knowing where dad is and that he is patiently waiting for the love of his life, my mom, as she recovers from this tragedy and continues to live a full life.

"She was no longer wrestling with the grief, but could sit down with it as a lasting companion and make it a sharer in her thoughts." ~George Eliot

Who will Speak for the Children?

Patricia Rogowski

The week had been almost euphoric. My husband, my daughter and I had 'road tripped' out to San Diego for the graduation of my daughter's fiancé from Marine boot camp.

The four of us spent a couple of days at the beach and then made our way back across the country via the Grand Canyon and other worthwhile sites. There was one site, however, we all wished we would have missed.

We were somewhere in Arizona when we stopped for gas and a potty break. As we pulled into the gas station, we heard yelling and cussing coming from another car in the lot. The brunt of the man's anger was being hurled at a little boy about nine or ten years old. The young mother sat stone-faced in the front seat. But when the man (and I use that term loosely) took a swing at the little boy, he dodged and bolted out of the car. Unfortunately, the little girl, probably four or five, was on the receiving end, instead.

All of this took place in a matter of seconds, while my daughter, future son-in-law, and I walked from the gas pumps and into the building. My husband, a police officer, was pumping our gas and assessing the situation to see if the man showed signs of turning on others at the scene. He was preparing to avert a potentially volatile situation.

My daughter and I were in the restroom when the mother came rushing in-carrying her little girl who was bleeding from her nose and lip. I felt sick to my stomach as I saw the fear and resignation in their eyes. No one should have to live like that, with a disgusting monster of a human being. As she was soothing her, telling her everything would be okay, the store clerk came in with a bag of ice and a towel, whispered that help was on the way, then turned and left.

I was torn. Should I say something? I wanted to so badly. If I didn't, I knew I'd never forgive myself. But what if the mother didn't want to hear what I had to say? What if I made her angry and her daughter had to witness yet another outburst from an emotionally wrought mother? I knew from having a sister caught in an abusive relationship for several years that making excuses for the actions of a bully of a man was part of being trapped in such a relationship.

I didn't have long to think about it though, because just as I had decided to say something, the man started pounding on the door, asking if the girl was okay and telling them to come out. I have to admit I was a bit frightened for my daughter's safety and my own. What if he came in? Would he turn his wrath on us? I had my own daughter's safety to consider, right? Thankfully my own selfish concerns were quickly replaced by compassion when I saw the fear in the eyes of mother and daughter, hearing his voice. She went to the door, opening it just a crack and told him they'd be out in a bit. She then turned her attention back to her little girl.

Knowing I had no excuse for staying any longer, I moved toward the woman, smiled and said, "You deserve better. And so do your children. It can stop now if you'll let it."

She smiled weakly, as my daughter and I walked out to leave, only to see the man trying to bully the clerk into going into the restroom to get his family for him. When my daughter saw this, she turned and went back into the restroom. I didn't know if she was getting scared or sick or what. The answer was 'none of the above'. She went back to tell them to stay there until help came and to please not leave with him.

The police arrived just as we were leaving, ready, willing and able to give an accurate account of what had taken place.

I have no way of knowing what the outcome was, but I do know that if I'd said nothing, I'd be a failure as a human being. Children don't ask to be born. But once they are, they have every right to expect to be safe and secure, to not have to be afraid that at any moment, the people who are supposed to protect them at all cost are the very ones they need to be protected from. And what about the little boy? Where is he? If someone didn't speak up for him, go after him, he could have be running forever.

> *"Injustice anywhere is a threat to justice everywhere."*
> ~Rev. Martin Luther King Jr.

I Love Camp More than I Hate Snakes

Melissa Row

I'd been spending a week at church camp every summer since I was seven. I loved that place. I still love that place. The kids, the counselors, the food, the fun, the music, and the classes – I loved it all.

The camp isn't fancy and it's located in the middle of nowhere. There's no air conditioning, we sleep on wood bunk beds in a wood building with a concrete floor, and the bathrooms are pretty primitive. We wouldn't have changed a thing. But the camp had a 'history' of sorts. When it was built back in the 1960's, there was an issue with copperheads. When building the chapel, they apparently disturbed a few nests of them. I guess it was quite an ordeal. But thankfully no one was hurt and the snakes were 'taken care of'.

Fast forward forty years. Some said it was the drought we were experiencing, others said it was the result of a housing development being built a couple of miles away; but for whatever reason, we were once again 'camp copperhead'. While it wasn't nearly as bad as it had been all those years ago, it wasn't unusual for the staff and camp manager to kill two or three a day.

They took several precautions to insure the safety of the campers – tennis shoes only, no night games, no exterior doors left open, bed checks and instructions on what to do if we saw a snake or were bitten by one. They even brought the conservation agent out to get his advice on how to handle the problem.

By the time the final week of camp came around (my week), things were much improved. There'd been only one snake sighting in the last six or seven days. The rules still remained in place, but because we were high school aged kids, they did allow us to have our night time prayer circles with our 'family groups' – we just had to do it under the canopy of the dusk to dawn lights.

It was the third night of camp. We were heading to the prayer circle area, when I stepped on my shoe lace and it came untied. I kept walking with the intention of retying it when I got there. When I got to the area where my group was gathered, I sat down on the ground to tie the shoe. But when I did, I felt a sharp little pinch or bite. I let out a little scream as I jumped up. A friend standing nearby with a flashlight shined it on me and there it was-the copperhead. And it had bitten me on the butt!

Talk about springing into action! The head counselor sent a camper for the nurse and another staff member to get the camp manager. I was made to stand with a belt cinched tightly around my waist. I could feel the bite area swelling and throbbing. It really hurt. I was feeling sick to my stomach and my heart was pounding. Everyone was great. We were all trying to keep each other calm.

My mom was called. She consented to have the manager drive me to the hospital rather than wait for the ambulance saying she would meet us there.

Wow! What a way to be remembered-the girl who got bit on the butt by a snake at camp. I could think of a lot better ways to be remembered, but I had to admit it was...memorable.

The doctor was pleased with the first-aid I'd been given. I had to have a shot of anti-venom and was told to take it easy for a few days. He said the bite would be painful for up to a couple of weeks, but that I'd be fine. I was relieved and thankful. But what about camp? I didn't want to miss the rest of camp. I couldn't!

My mom and the doctor insisted I spend the night at home where she could keep an eye on me. I would most likely be nauseated for a few hours and in pain. He also wanted her to be able to help control the swelling. But he agreed that if it was okay with my mom, that it would be fine to go back to camp the next day, provided I didn't do any running, swimming or anything else to exert myself. I could live with that.

So the next day-right before lunch-I returned to my beloved camp. The rest of the week went great even though I was now 'Snakebite Melissa'. But what made the whole event really memorable was the next year when some of my friends had t-shirts made for us to wear that said, "I was here when Melissa got bit on the butt by a snake. Where were you?"

"The antidote for fifty enemies is one friend."
~Aristotle

An Angel Named Joy

Grace Williamson

I knew I'd met the love of my life when I was sixteen. And three years later, when we got married, we did so knowing that a family might not be possible for us. We knew this because something else happened when I was sixteen; I was diagnosed with endometriosis – a condition that usually renders women infertile. I was told I might never be able to have a baby.

But thanks to the care of a wonderful doctor and a good deal of treatment and medication, John and I were thrilled to welcome our son into the world just weeks after our second anniversary. Three years later we were elated when we welcomed baby 'Boo' into our lives and the next year, our little Olivia. Take that, endometriosis!

A few months after Olivia was born, though, my nemesis came back with a vengeance. Pain, vomiting, fevers, chills...they were all a 'normal' part of my life, making it anything but normal. Three different doctors recommended a hysterectomy-all three agreeing the quality of my life would be significantly increased after the procedure. But I resisted. I wanted another baby.

For nearly five years I put up *with* the pain and put my family *through* the burden and aggravation of my health issues. John assured me he was perfectly willing to consider our family complete if it would mean I was healthier, but I wasn't ready to give up. I just didn't feel complete.

Throughout those years I prayed earnestly for God to give me another child. Why wasn't He answering my prayer? Was my family complete? Was I being selfish?

Yes, I decided I was…being selfish, that is. My health had deteriorated to the point I was struggling to take care of the wonderful husband and children I had. So after much soul-searching, I tearfully consented to the surgery.

The day I met with the doctor for pre-op blood work and consultation, I was an emotional wreck – so much so, that when the secretary called the hospital to schedule the surgery, I took the latest possible date the hospital's nurse gave as an option. I left feeling more unsettled than I'd ever been about anything. The hour-long drive home was spent crying so hard I had to pull over a couple of times to pull it together. I prayed for assurance that I was about to do the right thing. I told God that if He didn't want me to have the surgery He'd better let me know in no uncertain terms. I told Him I needed a lightning bolt experience.

John was working out of town that week, and when he called that evening, he could tell I was upset. Upset! That's putting it mildly. I was an emotional wreck! But as always, he was adamant that the decision was completely mine to make.

The next morning, I woke feeling much better. I felt that somehow everything was going to be okay. I felt as if a huge weight had been lifted off my heart. So, deciding to go on with my day, I went out to the garden to pick tomatoes, leaving the kids to finish brushing their teeth before joining me.

"Mom, somebody's on the phone for you." Seven year-old Boo hollered from the back door-toothbrush still in her mouth. "She says it's important."

I hurried across the yard and into the house. "Hello?"

"Good morning. This is Dr. Farris' office. I'm sorry, but I'm afraid we're going to have to make some changes in your surgery."

It's hard to say which was shaking more-my hands or my voice. "Really, why?"

The office manager I'd scheduled the surgery with the day before went on to tell me that she'd called the hospital first thing that morning to schedule a procedure for another patient and asked them to put it on the schedule right after mine. The nurse on the other end of the line told her that the operating room wasn't available that day, other doctors had all three rooms booked. The office manager told the nurse she'd spoken to a nurse named Joy the day before, and that she'd assured her it was on the schedule.

My head was reeling as she spoke. Was this my sign from God, or just wishful thinking? Was this my lightning? I didn't have to wait long for my answer, because in the next breath, the office manager said, "I don't know what's going on, but when I was told about yesterday's call, she said there was no one by the name of Joy that even worked on the floor – or in the hospital as far as she knew."

I could barely breathe. Joy had been there yesterday. I knew she had, but that she would probably never be there again – unless someone like me needed her. Joy was sent to bring me joy.

"I need to know what you want to do. When would you like to reschedule?"

"I don't," I said. I hung up after telling her I'd get back with her when I'd decided what to do.

Two weeks later, the day I was scheduled to have surgery, I took a pregnancy test. I was pregnant! I was pregnant the day I'd gone for the pre-op workup, but it was still too early to detect a pregnancy.

Had I gone ahead with the surgery, we would never have known our precious Emma even existed. We would never have known the beautiful, wonderful, funny, talented young lady who made our family complete. And I owe it all to Joy – the one who was sent to protect the life of my daughter.

Five months after Emma was born, I confidently went ahead with the surgery. I was ready and relieved to be able to enjoy good health and the joys of being a wife and mother.

"Insight is better than eyesight when it comes to seeing an angel." ~Quoted in The Angels' Little Instruction Book by Eileen Elias Freeman, 1994

What Happened in Mexico Should have Stayed in Mexico

Linda Harrop

Rebecca and I worked at the bank together. We were young, single, attractive, and, because it was the early 80s, if for no other reason, we were ready to take the world by storm.

I don't remember which of us thought of the idea first, but to us, taking a vacation together – to Mexico – sounded bold and exciting.

I'll never forget how euphoric it felt to look out the window of our room and see the beach just below. The sand, the sun and water…this was going to be a dream come true!

Mid morning the next day, we were on the beach soaking up the sun and went wading out into the ocean, when we got too hot, when Poco approached me. He looked to be in his early twenties, was definitely good looking and the fact that he was so clumsy with his English was completely endearing.

By the time he left, I'd learned he had just completed dental school, that was single, and that we'd be having dinner together later that evening.

Poco and I went out every night after that (with Rebecca's 'blessing'), dining, dancing, walking and talking along the beach. So on the last night of our stay, it didn't surprise me when he asked for my address so we could write to one another.

I didn't really expect to hear from him. That's why a couple of weeks later, when I received a letter from him in the mail, I was in shock. He asked me to write him back. I did. One letter led to another and another and another…. He told me he was in love with me and wanted to know if I felt the same.

Was I? How could I know something like that? How could he? We'd spent five evenings together struggling through language barriers to hold a conversation. Love needed more than that to grow. When I told him I didn't feel we could know that based on what we'd experienced, the letters stopped. I figured Poco would consider that my breakup and move on. What I didn't expect was what happened instead.

I'd been home from work a couple of hours and was getting ready to go for a run when the door bell rang. When

I went to the door, there was Poco. The same sweet smile, the same perfect haircut and the same soft eyes.

"What...what...how..." I was a stammering idiot.

His English much improved, he said he'd come so that he could prove to me that we were meant to be. Oh, and he wanted to be a dentist in the United States instead of Mexico.

Over the next few weeks we'd talk for hours, getting to know one another. We also poured over documents and paperwork trying to get permission for him to practice in the states.

The powers that be said there were two things stopping him from practicing dentistry in the US. One was the fact he hadn't produced licensure from Mexico and two was the fact he wasn't a citizen or legal resident. His excuse for not showing his license was that the Mexican government wouldn't cooperate because they needed dentists there and didn't want him to leave. Okay, plausible. His solution to not being legal was to get married.

Okay, I admit it...I was so starry-eyed and more naïve than I would have ever admitted. I said 'yes'. Despite the warnings and misgivings of my mom, sisters, friends, and even my boss, I said yes.

The first few months were great. He was the same Poco I'd been attracted to. But when he kept being denied permission to practice, he became discouraged and homesick. He wouldn't get a job, saying he was too good and too educated to have to do the kind of jobs people were willing to hire him for. But that didn't stop him from spending money – money we didn't have. He started staying out late and coming home drunk. That's the only time he wanted to have sex, so you can imagine how truly special and loved I felt, especially since he'd be wearing someone else's perfume.

A few days later I received a call from a local store saying he was trying to purchase several hundred dollars worth of clothing using my credit card. I was both angry and embarrassed. I didn't want to tell them he'd taken my card without permission, but we were getting in over our heads financially. I said no. The next morning I came to work with a black eye. My story was that I'd had to slam on my brakes and my sunglasses had done it when I hit my head on the steering wheel. I was so embarrassed and ashamed. How could I have been so naïve…so stupid? What was I going to do?

That night, I told Poco things had to change. He agreed and that he thought if he could go to Mexico and see his family, it would make all the difference in the world. He said he would get a copy of his license so that he could practice dentistry when he got back and we'd have the life we wanted. I agreed to give him that opportunity, saying the time apart would give us both an opportunity to get our heads on straight. Instead, he insisted I come with him.

In spite of the fact that Poco said his sister was preparing a special dinner in our honor, he and his family spoke Spanish the entire time and acted as though I wasn't there. I was very uncomfortable and began to feel ill. A few hours later I became violently ill. Poco appeared to be very concerned and insisted we go to the hospital. His sister, a doctor, said we could skip the preliminaries and go right to a room. I was so sick I didn't care or even try to make sense of it all.

Every time I'd think I was beginning to feel better, the nurse would come in to give me medication. She said I was having an allergic reaction to something I ate and that I needed the medication to get well. But each time she'd give it to me I would slip into a deep sleep.

For whatever reason, the nurse didn't come for hours and as the 'medication' wore off, I felt incredibly weak, but surprisingly coherent. As I looked around, I noticed there was nothing in the room. I remembered bringing my passport, insurance, and money with me that night. Where were they now? Where were my clothes? Why had the phone been removed? Where was Poco?

I managed to get out of bed with the intention of asking the nurse. When I got the door opened, the only person in sight was a middle-aged American woman named Marta. Thank you, Lord! She was an American missionary who volunteered at the hospital on a regular basis. She said they'd been instructed to not enter my room. That the patient was an elderly man who was dying, and wished to be left alone!

Thankfully she believed my 'story' and agreed to help me. The nurse eventually came to medicate me, but I faked taking it and falling asleep. She left after she was satisfied I'd be out for a while. Shortly after that, my 'missionary angel' sneaked back into my room, reporting that she'd found my clothes and purse in the patient lockers, but all identification, money and credit cards had been removed. Very quickly she told me she was going to create a diversion to get the nurse out of sight and that when she did I was to waste no time getting to the place she would meet me, and take me to safety.

I was terrified! What if something went wrong? What if she wasn't as nice as I was counting on her to be? I was worrying needlessly. Marta truly was my angel on earth. She not only helped me escape from the hospital, but she and her husband Greg went above and beyond to help me get through all the red tape it took to go home. Home – there really is no place like home.

My mother and sisters were frantic with worry. They said Poco had called them and told them we'd decided to live there permanently and that I wanted nothing more to do with them. They knew that wasn't true, but all attempts to contact me had failed. My mom insisted I see our doctor, who confirmed I still had low levels of poison in my system. Poco had been trying to kill me!

After regaining my strength, I found out Poco really wasn't Poco, that he'd never gone to dental school, that his sister was actually his wife and that she'd been in the country with him all along. The only positive in the whole mess was that I'd never really been married to him since he was already married.

The humiliation and embarrassment were almost overwhelming at times. But my family, friends and co-workers were such a tremendous source of strength. They could have said so many things, but instead, chose to say what I needed and longed to hear; that they loved me and would always be there for me.

Needless to say Rebecca and I didn't go back to Mexico. We decided the beach in San Diego was just as wonderful and a whole lot safer. It took a few years before I could even think about dating, but I did eventually.

I have now been married to my wonderful husband for almost twenty years and I am the mother of three beautiful daughters. None of whom, by the way, will ever be going to Mexico.

As for Marta and Greg, they are living back in the United States now, and are still a very important part of my life. Without them, I'd most likely not even have one.

"What we have done for ourselves alone dies with us; what we have done for others and the world remains and is immortal." ~Albert Pike

Chick o Stix

Tim Nelson

I was supposed to be a girl. After five boys, my parents wanted a girl, so the fact that I wasn't, meant I was a disappointment from the start. And not many days went by that I wasn't reminded of it one way or another.

Don't ever let anyone tell you little kids don't understand what's going on. When there's plenty of praise for everyone but you, when your dad goes to all your brothers' ball games except yours, when your brothers get an allowance for doing chores and you don't…you get the message loud and clear. Painfully loud and clear.

I remember waking up on Christmas morning every year hoping this would be the year I'd get Chick o Stix in my stocking. I loved those things. I still do. Every year I'd ask for a stocking full of them. And every year I'd think, 'well, maybe next year'.

I kept thinking if I got one more 'A' on my report card, ran faster, hit the ball harder, or did things without being asked that they'd love me more. Sometimes it seemed to work for a while. But usually it just seemed to make things worse.

When I was about seven, we moved into town. That's when Gene and Helen came into my life. They lived down the street from us. They were both teachers whose children were nearly grown. They asked my mom if my brothers, sister and I could go to a Bible camp their church was hosting. She said we could and from then on, we went to church every Sunday with Gene and Helen. They were the kind of people all kids should get to have for parents. With Gene and Helen, I felt like I counted for something – that I mattered.

Over the next few years things got progressively worse at home. My father was both emotionally and physically abusive, and my mom just let it happen. But since it was only me, I still thought I'd done something wrong – that since they didn't treat my brothers and sister that way, it must be something I was doing. In spite of the few people who knew my situation, telling me it wasn't my fault, I just couldn't believe it wasn't me.

They were parents – they wouldn't treat one of their kids like this unless they had a reason, right? So as an escape, I spent as much time as possible with Gene, playing sports or mowing grass and other odd jobs I could do; anything to get me out of the house.

When I was fourteen, three things happened. First, I realized that everyone else seemed impressed that I had a 4.0 GPA, that I had the fastest mile of anyone in 3a or 4a schools, and that I wasn't following in the not-so-nice footsteps of my older brothers. Everyone, that is, but my parents. Second, I got a part time job and finally had money to buy things I wanted until my parents found out and decided there was no need for them to spend their money on me; I was responsible for buying my clothes, shoes, school lunches, personal items...everything but the meals I ate when I was at the house. Third, I met Emma. I'd been going to church camp every summer since that first year Gene and Helen took me. Church and a relationship with God were important to me – it was some where and some thing that allowed me to feel better about myself. And Emma was always there, too. She was the prettiest girl I'd ever seen. Pretty, sweet, funny, and not afraid to just be herself, she made me smile. She made me feel like I was special.

I know most people don't find the person they're going to spend the rest of their life with when they're fourteen, but I did – or at least I hoped I had. But every time I started hoping, I'd hear my dad's voice saying what he always did;

137

that I was a no-good screw-up and that I'd never amount to anything. Why would anyone want to love someone like that?

As it turned out, though, Emma had noticed me. And she didn't think I was a screw-up. The day I found out she liked me was the first really happy day I ever remembered having. I knew in my heart, as long as I knew Emma cared, I could make it through anything.

It turned out that I got plenty of opportunities to find if that 'theory' was true or not. My dad became more and more abusive. I'd come to the house to find my clothes in the trash or other things I owned were missing. The physical abuse got worse – a couple of concussions and a couple of broken fingers.

The night I demanded my brother give back something he'd taken from me was the night my dad threatened to take my life and kicked me out of the house. It was also the first night of my new life. He told me to never come back, but he didn't have to. I knew no matter what I had to do, I was done being his victim. I was more scared than when he'd held that gun to my head, but in some strange way, it was a good feeling.

There was snow on the ground and it was in the teens that night. I slept in an abandoned house. It was cold, but at least it was dry and he wasn't there. Over the next two weeks I lived at school, a local fast-food place, the recreation center and on the street. I did a great job of hiding my situation from everyone, even Emma. My brother and sister would see me at school and act as if nothing had happened. They didn't even ask where I'd been staying. I was actually beginning to believe I could pull this off. But the night it was forecast to be twenty below zero, I knew I had to do something different.

So that day after school, I called Emma. "Emma, I have to tell you something, and I hope you won't be mad…." Emma knew what I'd been through growing up, we told each other everything. Or at least we had until now. Why would she want someone who was homeless? But as always, Emma was there for me. She started crying and telling me I could come to her house. She and her dad came and got me. That night I'd never felt warmer – inside or out. That night was the first night of my new life.

From that point on, Emma's family was my family as well. They'd been great up to that point, any way, but after that night, they assured me I would always have a home with them.

Some times I had difficulty believing I deserved to be so happy. I had Emma, her family loved me, and I didn't have to look over my shoulder to see if my dad was coming at me. That next Christmas was really special, too; I had a stocking full of Chick o Stix!

Emma and I were young – she was fifteen, I was seventeen. But we had a plan. By graduating early from high school, I could become a Marine and by the time she graduated, I'd be able to provide for us and she could go to college. We would be together forever.

The next year, that's exactly what I did. I left my beautiful Emma to go to San Diego to become a Marine. It was the hardest thing I've ever done, but I was proud of making it through. The day I graduated from boot camp, Emma and her parents – our parents – came to San Diego to be with me and to give me the best present ever. Emma was going to graduate early, too, and they were giving us their blessing for us to get married a year sooner than planned!

After graduation, I had a couple of weeks leave before starting the next phase of my training. So after making a vacation out of the trip back home, Emma and I went to see my parents. I wanted to see them – to find if maybe, just maybe, I'd finally made them proud.

My mom cried when she saw me. And while I know, in her own way, she does love me, it just isn't enough. As for my dad, well, he hadn't changed a bit. When Emma made the comment that, out of over a hundred candidates, I was one of only six to graduate a PFC rather than a private, he turned to her and said, "That won't last long. They'll bust his rank when he gets back out there and they see what a screw-up he is."

Wow! What a kick in the gut! But now I knew better. So I looked him straight in the eye, told both he and my mom that in spite of everything they'd said and done, I knew I wasn't a screw-up. I told them I was moving on and that I was done being their victim. And I've not looked back.

I don't wish my childhood on anyone. But in a few short months Emma will be my wife. And some day, when we have children of our own, I'll know how to be the dad my kids will deserve – thanks to the love her dad has shown me. Oh, and you can be sure they'll have a stocking full of Chick o Stix every year if that's what they want.

"They cannot take away our self-respect if we do not give it to them."

~Mahatma Gandhi

Enjoying the Simple Things in Life

The Surprise Wedding

Janet Evans

Wes and I could hardly keep a straight face the evening our youngest daughter, Delia, and her childhood sweetheart, Adam, left for dinner and a movie. We knew the 'movie' was actually going to be a marriage proposal in the park. Adam had called Wes several weeks ago asking permission to propose to Delia. He had just finished the final stages of training in the Marines, and would now be able to take Delia with him to live on base.

Both Wes and I were more than okay with the two of them getting married. They were young, yes, but if any two 'kids' deserved to be together, it was Adam and Delia. They'd been inseparable since Delia had been thirteen and Adam fifteen. He'd never left her side when she got a staph infection in the hospital from a simple tonsillectomy and had gone through counseling with her when she was attacked and nearly raped in a parking lot after work one night.

Delia had been there for Adam, as well. She'd seen him through some harsh and hurtful experiences that often come from a dysfunctional family such as his was. She had encouraged him and supported his dreams to become a Marine. She'd written multiple letters every day to make sure he would know she was praying for him and waiting for him at home when boot camp was over, and we'd all been there to share in his boot camp graduation. Yes, they deserved to be happy together.

The evening ended with lots of squeals of delight, hugs, kisses, happy tears, and the chatter of wedding plans. Life was good.

The next few weeks were filled with getting a date set, picking out a dress, deciding on decorations and all the things that go with a wedding. With the miles separating them, it wasn't easy, but both Delia and Adam remained upbeat and tried to focus on what was good rather than the fact that they couldn't be together. Skype didn't hurt, any, either.

We were in the countdown. The invitations were set to go out in the mail the following week when Wes and I came home from an evening out with friends to find Delia sobbing her heart out. Adam was being deployed to South Korea in thirty days. He'd be gone for six months to a year.

Words were useless. Nothing we could say was going to make her feel any better. She was heart-broken, angry, scared, disappointed and, most of all, she felt completely alone.

She was able to tell us that Adam would be coming home in less than two weeks and that he'd have two weeks at home with her before he had to leave. We assured her we weren't upset in regards to wedding plans being 'ruined', and that we'd do whatever we could to make their time together special.

Wes left the room while I was talking to Delia, but I didn't think much about it until later when he didn't seem all that upset about what had happened. When I questioned him, he just said he wanted to be strong for Delia.

It wasn't until just two days before Adam was due home that I understood why Wes was being so calm. While Delia and I were canceling flowers and food and photographers, Wes was arranging to have it all happen just as we'd planned, only sooner. I had just been to the bridal shop to pick up the veil we'd ordered. I didn't want Delia to see me crying – we'd done enough of that. Not wanting me to be upset, Wes spilled the beans. He and Adam had the whole thing planned out. Adam would take Delia out but instead of going where she thought they would be going, they would go to the church. Her dress, everything and everyone would be there waiting.

I couldn't believe it! My serious-minded, sometimes stoic husband had pulled off the biggest surprise anyone could possibly think of! And Adam had been in on it, too! They even had a honeymoon planned!

Now, could I manage to keep the secret? It wouldn't be easy, but surely I could manage for three or four days. I had to! I wouldn't ruin Wes and Adam's surprise for anything!

Delia was ecstatic over seeing Adam. She had told me more than once she was determined to make the most out of their time together, but it was obvious her anxiety and fear over him leaving and her sadness about the wedding postponement were going to get in the way.

The wedding was to take place two days after Adam arrived home, so that they'd have a week for a honeymoon and a few days to get military paperwork and such in order before he left. They had already applied for their marriage license, so that was taken care of. All that was needed was to get Delia to the church on time.

I fixed our regular family breakfast that Saturday morning which was to be followed with a trip to the farmer's market for me, yard work for Wes and Adam had said he'd like the two of them to go to the water park.

Delia didn't suspect a thing. She'd asked me to put her dress in my closet, so she wasn't aware that it was no longer in the house, the wedding party would be at the church dressed and ready for actions, the food was being delivered, our older daughter, Darcy, and son-in-law had decorated the church top to bottom...all we needed was the bride.

I will never forget the look on Delia's face when Adam brought her to the church. We arranged for Wes and me to be waiting in the parking lot so that we could see her reaction, as well. When they got out of the car, he took her hand and said, "Delia, I know it's usually not good luck for the groom to see the bride on their wedding day, but there could never be anything bad come from my looking at you. Right now you need to go with your mom, because we're getting married in a couple of hours. That is, if you want to."

"Yes, yes!" she sobbed. "I wanted to do this, so badly, but I didn't think I could ever begin to ask Mom and Dad to redo everything. They'd gone to so much trouble already." Still sobbing, Delia grabbed Adam, then her father, and then me.

Needless to say, Delia wasn't the only one crying at this point.

Realizing the clock was ticking, we went inside and started getting ready. Darcy wanted everything to be a surprise, so she wouldn't even let Delia peek at the decorations. But that was fine – just one more way to add a bit more magic to an already magical day.

There wasn't a dry eye in the place as Adam and Delia vowed to love one another 'til death do us part,' everyone knowing they were truly a 'match made in Heaven'.

Those tears turned to laughter, when after the minister pronounced them husband and wife, Adam grabbed her, gave her a kiss, and said, "It's about time. I thought this day would never come."

All too quickly, the days passed and it was time for Adam to leave. Delia is thankful for Skype and cell phones, but I'm sure she won't get a good night's sleep until Adam is home and they are together as they should be. Wes asked me the other day if I was up for planning a surprise homecoming for Adam when he returns early next year. I laughed and told him I'd consider it, but that I didn't know how he'd ever be able to top the surprise wedding.

"It takes hands to build a house, but only hearts can build a home."

~Author Unknown

Live for Today and Don't Worry About Tomorrow

Belle M. DuCharme

The words of a song from the 1960s floated through my head "la, la, la la la la, live for today and don't worry about tomorrow, yeah, yeah." Oh, yeah, this was a philosophy that I wrapped my mind around and lived from the time I graduated high school in 1966 until recently. Live in the moment, enjoy the wind in your hair, the blue in the sky, and the sand in your toes. Do I regret it? No. Do I wish I had planned better for the unexpected economical turn of events? Yes.

I did not start a retirement plan until I was fifty. I was divorced and raising my ten year old daughter without child support. Victoriously, I celebrated being able to purchase a two bedroom condo a mile from the California coast in Cardiff by the Sea. It was a short sale and it took me nine months to get a fixer property with holes in the bottom of the bathtub and large wine stains on the carpets. Funny, I loved the imperfections of that property the same as I had come to love my own imperfections.

Thirteen years later I had to sell that property after I lost my job due to the recession. I had too much debt and had made a couple of bad choices in purchases. Living beyond my means was a way of living in the moment for me. Living in the moment for me had to be redefined if I was to survive.

My world had changed and I was mentally adrift. In a span of two years, I lost my good paying position in a prestigious consulting firm to a layoff, my father passed away, my precious dog had to be euthanized, my home was too expensive for me to keep, and my health was challenged with a surgery for diseased ovaries and a surprise appendectomy.

For a moment I was afraid. I asked myself, "What do I do now? Who will want an old worker like me?" But that moment passed as I rallied my defenses and said out loud, "I will not retire from this life without a fight." And the fight started with the sale of my property in Cardiff by the Sea. My father had always said that "location, location, location" was what mattered in the value of real estate and he was right. My property sold all cash in less than a week. I had lost thirty percent of the equity value but luckily I had enough to downsize to an affordable home in the back country of San Diego County called Sunshine Summit. Just the name "sunshine summit" made me feel positive. I paid down my debt and socked some away in my retirement fund. After a year of unemployment, I realized I had to accept less pay and go back to doing work that I used to do when I was younger. I can not work physically at the same level I could in the past but my wisdom and experience in my field has created far more opportunities than I imagined.

Today at age sixty-three I celebrate the moments of my life, the graduation ceremony at U.C. Berkeley for my daughter, my son's decision to start up his own business, and the birth of my grandsons.

I am sitting here looking out my window at the billowing thunderheads rising above the mountains against the bluest of skies. I am living for today and in the moment but I am more prepared for tomorrow. I have rewritten the song and it now goes, "la la la la la la live for today and look forward to tomorrow, yeah, yeah."

> *"The bamboo that bends is stronger than the oak that resists."* ~Japanese Proverb

Albert

Mae Baas

Most kids have pets – a dog, cat, fish, hamster, guinea pig or something else in the 'domesticated' category. But my kids weren't 'normal' when it came to pets. We're farmers, so we were always heavy in the pet department.

At any given time, we had a dog or two, cats who lived in the barns, frogs, guinea pigs, salamanders (really cool), and our favorite livestock. We even rescued a baby mouse from a sack of feed and kept it as a pet; that is until the little 'darling' got loose in the house. Did I hear someone say mouse trap?

In addition to the sheep we raised, when the kids were small, they'd always have a bottle-fed calf to raise and take to the fair for the calf show.

Olivia (second youngest) was three the summer she made her debut in the show ring. She worked diligently alongside me to make sure her calf, Albert, would be ready for the fairs. She'd fed and watered him, led him around the barn lot on a halter, brushed him and treated him with as much love as other kids would have a new puppy. It was actually pretty impressive to see someone as young as she was, having the attention span she did. She and Albert made quite a team.

Once the fairs were over for the summer, Albert was turned out with the sheep to graze. You see, once the kids were done showing their calves, they'd be fed out, butchered and put in the freezer for our year's meat supply.

None of the kids had ever had a problem with this; they understood the realities of farm life. They weren't unfeeling or uncaring, they simply understood the natural cycle of livestock. All except Olivia, who was a bit more sensitive than her older siblings. She was the one who later rescued the mouse from the feed sack. It would even be fair to say she was a bit of a drama queen at times...but in a humorous sort of way. Olivia could have easily played the role of Fern in "Charlotte's Web".

When it was time for Albert to go to that 'great big pasture in the sky' by way of the butcher (my husband), I told Olivia it was time to say good-bye to Albert. We told her that Albert was big enough now to be meat and that's what he needed to do. So, in typical Olivia fashion, she said goodbye with hugs and kisses, words of adoration, a handful of feed for the road, even a freshly picked flower tucked in his halter. But thankfully, no tears or pleas for pardon. Whew...one hurdle crossed.

A couple of weeks later, when the meat was packaged and ready for us to pick up, Olivia went along with us to pick it up. It's not like going to the grocery store to pick up a few things, though. We're talking about 450 pounds of meat, so it takes a while to get it all loaded and then unloaded and into the freezer when we get home.

I noticed Olivia was quieter than usual on the ride home and later, as well, while John and I filled the freezer. I interpreted this as the proverbial 'other shoe' about to drop. But I decided to let her alone with her thoughts. I knew that if she had something she wanted to say, she'd say it. She always did. And the fact that we were going to be enjoying hamburgers for supper – courtesy of Albert – would be the perfect opportunity for her to speak her mind.

That evening, during dinner, the older kids were talking about spelling tests, lunchroom antics, and who said what to who when all of a sudden Olivia held up her burger, looked John straight in the eye and asked, "Is this Albert?"

I thought John, who was normally unshakeable, was going to need CPR. But he made a quick recovery, looked at me, then looked at Olivia and said, "Yes, honey, it is."

Olivia took another look at the burger in her little hand, took a little bit, chewed it thoughtfully (and surprisingly, tear-free), then said with a huge smile on her face… "Well, he tastes pretty good, don't he?"

It was now mine and John's turn to smile. Olivia 'got it'. She understood the purpose of livestock. She had allowed reason to win out over emotion, even when it came to her 'pet'. She understood that while animals can be called and considered pets, they are still animals and have a purpose to serve, especially in the world of agriculture. Not bad for a preschooler, is it?

"Life is what we make it, always has been, always will be." ~Grandma Moses

Less is Definitely More

Leah Weissmuller

The kids wouldn't even come out of their rooms the day we had the yard sale. They were so angry over having to sell what we'd deemed unnecessary. But when you're nine, twelve, and fourteen, everything you have is necessary in your eyes.

But we didn't have a choice. We'd purchased the house ten years ago-at a time when things were more than good for us financially. Thanks to Eric's aggressive approach when it came to investing, we'd enjoyed exotic vacations, the best clothes, private school for the kids...we were living a lifestyle most people only dream of. But we're living proof that dreams can quickly become nightmares.

The economic meltdown began and our bank accounts did the same. We were partners with another couple in a real estate business located in Florida – one of areas hit hardest by the recession. People were losing their jobs (and houses) right and left. So naturally our business suffered as well.

In spite of all the money we had (most of which was actually only on paper) we'd grossly over extended ourselves to the point of no return. To get out with at least a shred or two of dignity, Eric and I decided to sell anything and everything we could, pack up the kids and start over.

We worked with the bank and other creditors to reduce and consolidate our debts on everything but the house. The house, thankfully, we were able to sell to the administrator of one of the hospitals, but for much less than it was worth and almost twenty thousand less than we still owed. The bank, seeing that as pocket change in comparison to other delinquent mortgages, was willing to write off 50%, leaving us with a manageable sum to repay if we were able to find jobs wherever we ended up going.

We ended up in Texas, where Eric got a job teaching business at a public high school – the one our children would eventually attend. I went to work in the marketing department of the local medical center. It wasn't the type of writing I was used to doing, but it was enjoyable and the people were nice to work with.

The kids were miserable at first. Public school was quite a bit different than they were used to. And in the world of sports teams and the drama club, they were nobody here. We went from living in a house of over 3,000 square feet to one of just under 2,000. Instead of going to the movies, mall, or sports club whenever they were bored with their computer games, they put a movie in the DVD player. And as for computer games, we had a family time schedule to use the one laptop we kept.

Eric and I kept thinking they'd adjust – that we all would – but instead of getting easier, it just seemed to get harder. The car we'd kept got hit in the parking lot of the school, Evan's tooth got broken on the playground at school (we didn't have dental insurance) and the kids got to the point that all they did was sit in their rooms doing nothing – not even homework – which really began to show in their grades.

I hated what was happening to my family. Not so much the things we no longer had, but the toll the move was taking on my children's emotional health and their self-esteem. I knew we had to do something before it got any worse. I just wasn't sure what that something was.

After discussing the situation with Eric, we decided to speak to the guidance counselor at the high school where Eric taught. She was extremely helpful in giving us ideas on how to help the kids adjust to their new lifestyle and surroundings. She said that by investing ourselves into new hobbies and interests rather than dwelling only on the old ones, we'd establish ourselves here and learn to be confident and happy again.

It wasn't easy at first, but before too long, Drake and Eric both discovered a love for tennis, Evan joined 4-H and won a blue and a red ribbon on his wood-working projects and after practically dragging Marley through the flea market with me (I was looking for a cheap but pretty vase), she discovered she loved the look of vintage costume jewelry.

Using some of her birthday money from grandparents, she bought a couple of inexpensive items, revamped them a bit and when she wore them to school, all the other girls wanted to know where she'd gotten them. My entrepreneur was born!

Don't get me wrong, it wasn't an overnight success. The kids still missed their old life, but as they started to believe in themselves again, others did, too. We all started to see the value of having less instead of more; of realizing that the real value of someone was determined by what they were inside instead of where they lived, what they wore, or what latest and greatest gadget they had.

I think the real turning point was when our former business partners came by after visiting the university their daughter was planning to attend, which was about an hour from where we lived. Being a bit older, they'd been more financially secure than we had and had weathered the storm with little more than giving up a few vacations and the condo on the beach. After the initial 'it's been too long' greeting, things were awkward. They obviously pitied our 'sub-standard' living conditions and I overheard their daughter, who Marley had once idolized, ask Marley how she was able to even get a date if she had nothing to wear but 'that'.

I held my breath waiting for Marley to burst into tears or agree with Dawson and seek out pity for her unfortunate life. But she did neither. Instead, she said, "Things are different here. Here people are more concerned about how nice you are and just being yourself instead of how much money you have." And then she finished with, "It's really pretty cool."

That night over dinner (our friends had made an excuse for not staying to eat with us) we talked about how much things had changed over the last year and how that after we'd quit fighting those changes, things were actually better. No, we didn't have a lot of stuff, but we knew each other better, we knew ourselves better, we had friends who didn't care about what we did or didn't have, and we were happy.

"Be content with what you have, rejoice in the way things are. When you realize there is nothing lacking, the whole world belongs to you."
~Lao Tzu

The Christmas Tree

Emily Murphy

Christmas. I usually looked forward to the holidays. I loved decorating the house, inside and out. I loved the shopping, the caroling, filling the stockings after the kids and grandkids went to bed, getting together with family and friends...I loved it all.

But not this year. The year had been a difficult one. John had been with the same company for twenty-seven years and was looking forward to retiring the next year. But due to poor investments and mismanagement, the company had folded, taking most of his retirement with them.

Out of a job, with basically no retirement left, we didn't know which way to turn. Yes, it was true he was retiring several years before 'normal' retirement age, but he was too old to be able to start over, building a retirement account from scratch. I'd always worked part-time, but my salary had been our 'fun money'. Things were going to have to change.

After taking a long look at the situation, we'd decided to down-size; sell the house and get something more modest and more efficient to heat and cool. The taxes and insurance would be less, too, lowering our expenses. We would drop the television plan we had, we didn't need all those channels, we'd reduce our cell phone plan, quit eating out so much and cut back on how much we spent on gifts for Christmas.

Surprisingly the house sold quickly, only two months on the market. It was in a great neighborhood and school district, but even at that we were thrilled and shocked with the market being what it was at the time....

As I started pulling the Christmas decorations out of the attic of the new (and much smaller) house, I ran out of room to put possessions away before I ran out of things to decorate with. And somehow it just didn't look the same here.

Our youngest son was the only one left at home. When he saw what I was doing, he said he and his girlfriend, Charlie, would help decorate the tree when they got back from taking their turn ringing the Salvation Army bells with the youth group at church.

Ryan had been a bit sad about leaving the only home he'd ever known, but taking the practical approach that was so typical of Ryan, he'd said he understood completely, that we had to do what was best for our future.

As I was stringing the lights on the tree, I was almost relieved I wouldn't have to decorate it. Ryan and Charlie would enjoy that process and I could go on, not having to think about how great it used to look next to the fireplace.

Right after lunch, Ryan and Charlie came in laughing and carrying flavored hot chocolates from the quick stop. They'd brought one for John and me, too. John had gone to help his brother with a project, but we knew he'd enjoy the festive drink later on.

Pointing to the boxes of ornaments, I said, "Have fun. I think I'll go read for a while."

"No, don't go," Charlie and Ryan said together. "Help us."

Sighing, I sat down and began to unwrap the ornaments, handing them to the kids.

"Who made this?" Charlie asked.

One by one, as each ornament was taken out, we talked about who had made or given it to us. The crayon-colored paper holly done by Rachel in pre-school, the bread dough star and wreath Trina made in second grade, Ryan's sequin-covered satin balls that seemed to unravel a little more each year, the three '1st Christmas Together' ornaments John and I had been given as wedding gifts thirty years ago, each of the kids' 'First Christmas' ornaments, and Tim's paper angel scribbled with blue and yellow crayon that had topped our tree since he'd made it when he was two; twenty-six years ago.

As I told the 'story' behind each of my treasured ornaments, it dawned on me that the tree was more than just a Christmas tree. It was the story of my life, the important part, any way. It didn't matter what kind of tree I had or what kind of house it stood in. The ornaments on the tree were what made it special. And the same held true for the house we lived in and what I could or couldn't give my family for Christmas.

That was three Christmases ago. I look forward to decorating the tree just like I used to. But this year, I'm even more excited about giving Ryan and Charlie their 'Our 1st Christmas' ornament for the tree they'll put in their apartment.

Things haven't always been easy, but we've got everything we need and are blessed with a beautiful family and lots and lots of love.

"Rejoice with your family in the beautiful land of life!" ~Albert Einstein

Love Soup

Millie Gaulin

My daughter called one morning to ask if she could come over to talk. I could tell by the tone of her voice something was wrong, but since she didn't come out and say anything, I didn't want to pry. I assumed I'd hear about it in a couple of hours when she got here.

Sassy (short for Cassandra) and I had a great relationship, but she wasn't the type to bring her problems to me, so I couldn't help but be worried.

"Mom, I think my marriage is over," she blurted out.

"Why do you think that?" I asked, alarmed.

Sassy went on to tell me how things had gone bad with a couple of projects her husband was working on and as a result he'd lost out on a promotion at work. And what was even worse was the position he was in was most likely being eliminated. She went on to say because he hadn't confided any of this to her initially, she'd been less than understanding when she'd opened the mail to find a few late notices, because he'd not paid some of the bills.

On top of that, Sassy said, she was pretty sure he'd gone out for lunch with one of the women in his office more than once.

"Mom, I can't compete with all of that."

"So that's it," I asked? "You're ready to give up just like that? Honey, marriage is hard work. I'm not coming to Michael's defense, but if you love your man, you have to fight both with and for him. What you need is a big pot of love soup."

"Love soup?"

"Love soup. You've had it a lot of times. You know, it's got beef broth, onions, carrots, corn and..."

"Oh, that? I thought that was just what you threw together when you didn't feel like cooking."

I then proceeded to tell Sassy how love soup came to be a part of our family's history:

I told her how my parents had gotten married in the spring of 1929. My grandfather had given them a plot of land as a gift; one that would allow him to provide for his family, for them to build their farming operation on; possibly even joining it with theirs.

If you know anything about history, you know that 1929 was the year of the infamous stock market crash and the beginning of a period of desolation and desperation for many people around the world.

Over the next three years, my parents added two additional mouths to feed to their family but more often than not, there was next to nothing to feed them with. The result? Love soup. My mother eked out every bit of flavor she could get from the neck bones she'd get from the market for next to nothing. Combining them with a bit of salt, onions and whatever else she grew in their little garden. More water than anything, she always served the soup saying it might not have many vegetables in it, but that was because it was so full of love.

Throughout the depression, the years of rationing during WWII, and whenever else times were tough, emotionally or otherwise, she'd make a pot of love soup. She'd never add more than she had originally, saying they still needed more love in it than anything else.

"So why did you fix it, Mom?"

"Whenever money was tight, or your dad and I didn't see eye to eye, or you kids were more challenging than we could handle, I'd make a pot. And you know what, it always worked. Things were always better after we'd eaten a pot of love soup."

I sent Sassy home with a hug, a kiss, and a couple of beef bouillon cubes.

That was nine years ago. Sassy and Michael have regular love soup nights at their house…with their three children. See, it really works.

"Love is the greatest refreshment in life."
~Pablo Picasso

Motherly Sacrifices

Jackie Tucker

Growing up in the Ozarks during the early 1920s wasn't like anything most people today could even imagine. My folks farmed 360 acres and raised nine of us kids on love and hard work. And there were always other mouths to feed, as well. An aunt, uncle, and three cousins who'd fallen on hard times stayed for several weeks, the traveling preacher always stayed with us when he was in the area, family that came from St. Louis to visit...always someone.

Mom and Dad were always going above and beyond to make sure everyone had what they needed, too. I don't know how they did it. Mom made all our bread, butter, cream... everything from scratch. She made most of our clothes, for years she was either pregnant or nursing a baby, washing diapers...and people today think there aren't enough hours in the day!

But of all the things she did, nothing sticks out in my mind more than her nut picking. Every fall when the walnuts fell from the trees, Mom would have some of us kids gather them – lots and lots of them – and lay them out behind the chicken house to dry. After the hulls fell off them, we'd have to gather them up again in buckets. Then each night after she was done with her day's work, Mom would sit in her rocking chair with a little hammer, the shoe last and nail, cracking and picking out those walnuts. She'd sit down to start cracking and picking just before dark and still be working when we'd go to bed.

If you've never had the pleasure of picking walnuts, then you can't even begin to understand how tedious a task it is. But Mom was careful to get the meats out in as large a chunk as possible. And they were clean; meaning pieces of the shell weren't mixed in. She'd fill pint-sized mason jars with the nut meats, leaving the lid off them for a day or two so any excess moisture wouldn't cause them to mold, once sealed.

We'd keep a few of the nuts for ourselves to have for baking and an occasional treat in our oatmeal, but the main reason Mom worked so hard to pick so many nuts out was for us kids.

Mom sold the nuts to her brother, Alphonse, who ran the store in our little community. You might actually say she traded the nuts. She traded them for Christmas candies and a little trinket for each of us. Just thinking about it now brings tears to my eyes. I am humbled when I think of the hours and hours she spent just so we'd have a scant handful of hard candy and a barrette or ribbon for our hair and comb or shaving soap for my older brothers. And even though I was an obedient child, I am ashamed to think of what I could have done to show my thanks, but didn't.

As I grew older, I continued to see Mom's giving spirit. And a few years later, when I got married and had a family of my own, I would often be reminded of my mom and how she gave of herself so unselfishly. I had plenty of opportunities to be the kind of mother my mom was. Instead of cracking and picking walnuts, I picked as many blackberries as I possibly could each summer to make jelly that I sold to a store in the town twenty miles away.

Times have changed, though. Mothers today don't pick blackberries or walnuts in order to give their kids the Christmas they want to give them, but what hasn't changed is the fact that a mother's heart is an unselfish heart; one that will go with a lot less sleep, without a new pair of shoes or that manicure she'd love to have for the sake of her child's needs and wants.

Mom's been gone for over thirty years now. But as long as any of us kids are alive, the memory of her tiny little fingers working with such love will be very much alive.

"What greater thing is there for human souls than to feel that they are joined for life - to be with each other in silent unspeakable memories."

~George Eliot

Tough Minds, Tough Bodies, Tough Hearts

There's No Way Around But Through

Mark Rickerby

When I was about thirteen years old or so,
I was walking through the hallway to class
When the school bully stood in front of me
And absolutely refused to let me pass.

I moved to the left and then to the right.
He just laughed and moved that way, too.
It was that moment when it dawned on me
That there was no way around but through.

So I kicked the bully right where it hurts.
He let out a yell and I watched him fall.
After that, he gave me plenty of room
When he saw me coming down the hall.

I really should try to remember his name,

Maybe send him a "thank you" card.
Because without the lesson he taught that day,
My life might have been very hard.

You see, a big bully doesn't have to be human.
It's whatever keeps you and your goal apart.
So much talent is forever lost to the world
Because of the bullies that hide in the heart.

So whatever it is that stands in your way
That keeps you from living a life that's true,
Remember the lesson I learned from the bully.
My friend, there's no way around but through.

'Don't be discouraged. It's often the last key in the bunch that opens the lock." ~Author Unknown

Near-fatal Attractions

Abbie Donnelly

I left home at seventeen to start my college career. I was going as an agricultural science major, not what I'd planned to do, but because of my family's prominent farming background and the scholarships that came as a result, I thought, 'Hey, why not?'.

The transition from high school to college is huge on its own, but when you add trying to be someone you're not and doing something you don't have a heart to do, the stress takes its toll. And in my case, it was just one big train wreck.

After one semester I was miserable, making poor decisions, failing classes and struggling to keep my head above water. Somehow I made it through and then tried to take the summer to reconnect with who I really was. I made the decision to switch schools and majors. I felt I was back on track. I was...for a while.

But when I went back to school that fall, I just couldn't catch a break. I had to have surgery for kidney stones, the place I worked closed, and I still felt empty. I felt like that fish out of water everyone always talks about. I knew something was wrong, but when the solution didn't come quickly, I started looking in all the wrong places for the answer. I partied when I knew that was the last thing I needed. I went out with a guy I didn't like but, hey, it was something to do, right? Wrong!

Our first date was a movie and innocent enough, so no big deal. The second date was okay, but when it was over, he did a recap of the evening; he told me everything I'd done 'wrong'. The third date was a repeat of the second. I'm the first to admit I didn't have my head on straight but even I was smart enough to know this wasn't going anywhere I needed or wanted to go.

When he called the next day, I told him I was struggling in school (the truth) so I had decided that I just didn't want to date anyone until I was back on track. I wasn't being totally honest, when I told him it was nothing against him. Something told me that this was the best way to handle the situation. To say he didn't take it well is an understatement.

Over the next few days, I'd come out to my car after work or class to find notes on my windshield. Sometimes I even found him waiting for me. He called constantly, asking who I was with and what I was doing. He even started showing up where I worked for no reason other than to watch me.

I tried a few different strategies to get him to leave me alone. I tried just treating him as a friend, ignoring him, and finally, I asked him to leave me alone. I told him I didn't appreciate the way he was stalking me and I wanted him to stop. He got angry, saying he'd go anywhere he wanted any time he wanted. He grabbed my arm and gave me the most venomous look I'd ever seen, and dared me to stop him.

I knew I was in way over my head. I wanted to call my mom so badly. We'd always been so close, I still considered her my best friend. But I was so ashamed of the way I'd been living. I thought I was doing a pretty good job of hiding it all from her and my dad. I didn't want to disappoint and hurt her, so I didn't call. Instead, I just stayed in the denial neighborhood of la-la land where I thought I could handle things on my own.

I went on to class that night, but when I got home, I found him sitting in my apartment waiting for me, he'd come in through a window. I tried as hard as I could to hide the fear I felt. I tried to talk him out but he had other things on his mind.

I spent the next several minutes being thrown against the walls of my apartment, getting my face punched and getting kicked repeatedly in the ribs and the stomach. When I tasted blood in my mouth, all I could think about was the fact that my parents had spent thousands of dollars they didn't have to give me a beautiful smile. This was how I was thanking them.

When beating me was no longer fun, he started trying to rip my clothes off. That's when I decided he was not going to break me. I fought back with energy and might I didn't know I possessed. Finally, I was able to get out the front door of my apartment, down the stairs and into the street. He took off in his truck, but I knew this wasn't over.

First of all, I called a friend to come stay with me. Then I called my mom and dad. I told them everything, the good, the bad, and the ugly. My dad, a state policeman, went into 'cop mode' and ordered me to the local police station to file charges against him and start proceedings for a restraining order. My mom said she'd be there in a couple of hours. Overall they were great. They were hurt, yes, but they knew I'd learned some very hard lessons and there were more serious issues at hand.

As it turned out, this guy came from a wealthy family, had been in quite a bit of trouble for other things and couldn't afford to have anything else on his record. So when I filed charges and requested a restraining order, his dad hired a lawyer to try to discredit me and get the whole incident excused or erased.

What should have been a single (but very frightening) court appearance turned into three court appearances, being put on the stand and grilled by his lawyer and listening to 'witnesses' tell lie after lie about me and the supposed relationship I was in with their decent up-standing citizen of a friend.

This process dragged out over several months, during which I dropped out of school, couldn't keep food down, went from 120 pounds to less than 100 pounds, was constantly followed by his friends, almost ran down in a parking lot by his friends, and had to call the police to my apartment on several occasions because of threatening letters, messages written in fake blood on my windows, and rocks thrown through my window.

Not able to leave my apartment without looking over my shoulder, turned into being afraid to leave at all. I did leave, but the psychological damage of the attack is powerful and as painful as the attack itself. I'd been victimized but I was the one feeling like a prisoner.

In the end, the judge was wise enough to see though him and ordered the restraining order to stand. But I knew that wasn't enough. The temporary one hadn't deterred him, why should I believe this one would be any different? I would never be safe as long as I was anywhere he could find me. So I left.

Without telling anyone where I was going, I found a job several hundred miles away. My parents came to help me pack what few belongings we could get in our vehicles and I left to start a new life.

Today, I am happily married to a wonderful Christian man and have a thriving career in a field I'd never even considered. We own a lovely house that is truly a place to call 'home', and I'm finally able to go places without looking over my shoulder. The journey hasn't been easy, or without its scars. Because of the beating I took that night, I'm unable to have children. I'm still dealing with the guilt of my poor judgment and the price my husband and I will pay for the rest of our lives. But we'll be fine. We know there are children out there who need to be rescued and loved; children who need a second chance at life – much like the one I got.

"We acquire the strength we have overcome."

~Ralph Waldo Emerson

Christmas in February

Teresa Perry

When the report came back that my husband had colon cancer, we stayed surprisingly calm. Our doctor assured us it was in the earliest stages and was completely treatable; that surgery would most likely be all that was necessary to take care of it. No chemo or radiation, just the surgery. Feeling confident, we scheduled the operation for the Monday after Thanksgiving.

The doctors were right; the surgery was a complete success and no further treatment would be necessary. He was doing so great. So well, in fact, that the doctor released him to come home a day earlier than planned.

I answered the phone that Wednesday morning as I was finishing up my morning coffee. "Tessie," he said, "you can come get me. They're letting me out of here."

"Alright, I'll bring some clothes and be there within the hour." As I said a prayer of thanks, I smiled knowing Ralph would be home with me in just a short while.

When I stepped off the elevator onto the floor his room was on, I knew immediately something was wrong. You could feel the tension. One or two of them looked up at me and then quickly looked back down. It wasn't until I saw one nurse practically running out of Ralph's room that I got that sick feeling in my stomach. She stopped short when she saw me, came slowly toward me, and asked me to come with her.

We went back into Ralph's room – it was empty.

"Where's my husband?" I didn't even try to hide the panic in my voice.

"When I went in to take his vitals about twenty minutes ago, he was just hanging up the phone. I started to take his temperature when he said he wasn't feeling well all of a sudden. I noticed he was really pale and sweating, so I turned to put the thermometer down and was going to get his pulse. But he collapsed on the bed before I could even get to him. He coded, but we were able to bring him back. They've taken him to ICU. If you want to come with me, the doctor would like to talk to you."

I couldn't believe what I was hearing. He'd been fine less than an hour ago. They said he'd coded. Didn't that mean his heart had stopped beating? Yes, that's exactly what it meant. The doctor said he'd been without oxygen for almost five minutes. Even I knew that was long enough to cause serious damage. I was so busy trying to sort everything out in my head that I barely heard the doctor say I needed to call my family.

"What?" I said. My family? Why did he say that? Did he think Ralph was going to die? He said there were decisions that needed to be made.

When I was finally allowed in to see him, I hardly recognized the man I'd been married to for over fifty years. His skin was a horrible shade of gray, in some ways he didn't even look real. He had multiple machines hooked to him, an IV and a respirator in his mouth, he wasn't doing well breathing on his own.

The doctor told me the next few days were critical, that every day he was on the respirator his chances of ever being able to breathe on his own were greatly reduced. And because he was still in a coma, it was impossible for him to take respiratory therapy. It turns out that the decisions he'd referred to a few minutes earlier were whether or not to unplug him and let him go. As I very politely but firmly told the doctor, there were no 'decisions' to be made.

Three weeks passed before he became cognizant. He was naturally disoriented, but without being able to speak, it was hard to tell if he had suffered any effects from being without oxygen for so long. They tried to take the respirator out three or four times, but each time they did, Ralph would become so agitated and panicky trying to breathe on his own that he'd come close to hurting himself. Even though it sounded a bit barbaric, I asked if they could restrain him until he became acclimated to breathing on his own again. Their response: looking at me like I had three heads. But he didn't want it in either, and tried to remove it himself a couple of times. Their decision: mildly sedating him. He was living in a stupor.

The kids were great; encouraging and supporting me, not wanting to give up on their dad. Our church family was there to sit with me, pray with me and do whatever else they could do to make the long days as pleasant as possible. But the weeks passed by, Christmas came and went like any other day of the week, and Ralph was still unable to breathe on his own.

A few days after the New Year, the doctors told me they felt Ralph's condition had reached a plateau – that he wasn't going to get any better. They suggested I consider putting him in a nursing home. They said they would not be able to justify keeping him much longer. This meant our insurance and Medicare wouldn't be paying much longer.

My reply was an emphatic, 'No!' While I was pleased with the care Ralph had been given and the way I'd been treated all those weeks, I wasn't completely comfortable with the doctors' attitude about the respirator. I just didn't think they'd tried hard enough.

We had been told about a doctor who practiced in a city about a hundred miles away who had experience with cases similar to Ralph's. After talking with him on the phone, we felt hopeful, euphoric even; enough so as to transfer Ralph to the hospital where Dr. 'K' was on staff. After reading his file and doing his own examination, Dr. 'K' looked at me and said he was completely confident he would have Ralph breathing on his own in less than a week and sitting up and talking in less than a month.

Five days later Ralph was respirator free. Less than two weeks later, on February ninth, I heard my husband say my name for the first time in more than two months. I didn't know whether to laugh or cry, so I ended up doing both. It was the most beautiful sound in the world!

After he said my name, he asked if I'd finished the Christmas shopping. I laughed and said, "No, not yet."

Following Dr. K's advice, we waited a few days before we started giving Ralph any details about what had transpired over the last ten weeks. The trauma could have adversely affected his progress. When we did tell him, though, he was shocked and understandably confused and upset, but for the most part, handled it well. His biggest concern was that the little ones, our grandchildren, had missed out on Christmas. So we had Christmas. It was February, but we had Christmas, and it was the best ever.

"The only rock I know that stays steady, the only institution I know that works is the family."

~Lee Iacocca

A Shower? That Would be Lovely

Emma Skov

I'd just hit 'send' to submit an article to one of the publishers I worked for. I felt good about it being a week ahead of deadline and felt confident they'd be pleased with what I wrote. I turned around to get up out of my chair when the first wave of nausea hit.

"Oh," I said to my daughter, who had come to ask me a question, "I don't feel so well all of a sudden."

I tried to stand up when another wave of nausea hit along with the all too familiar pain of kidney stones. I'd suffered (and I do mean, suffered) with chronic kidney infections and kidney stones since I was fourteen. In twenty-five years, I'd had countless rounds of antibiotics for infection, eight surgeries to remove stones, several lithotripsy treatments. I had also passed several stones without medical intervention.

I told my daughter what was happening and asked her to help me to the bathroom. My husband was working and I didn't want to bother him. It wasn't as if I'd never been through this before. I just needed to take some pain medication and some rest, hoping I could pass the pesky little thing.

Fortunately she didn't listen to me. She called her dad, who came home and took me to the ER. Tests confirmed what we knew, a kidney stone. But unlike the other times, I had a temperature of over 104 and I was lethargic. That, combined with an almost non-existent white count revealed I was septic; I had an often fatal condition known as septicemia or blood poisoning because of my body's response to the kidney stone and the infection built up around it.

I vaguely remember them moving me to a room and inserting an IV with several different bags of medication, hooking up a heart monitors, and other paraphernalia and covering my face with an oxygen mask.

A few hours later, having been assured I would be fine, my husband left to go home so our daughter wouldn't be in the house alone all night. I remember him kissing me goodnight, but having to lift that mask to do it.

A short while later a nurse, who was wearing a cloth mask over her mouth, came to check my vitals. When she did, she immediately called for help and began asking me if I knew my husband's phone number. I must have told her the number because she picked up the phone and I heard her telling him to come back right away, that I'd taken a serious turn for the worse and they were taking me to ICU.

I spent the next three days in a semi-coma. I did regain consciousness for a few moments that first night and can remember my husband's tear-stained face, him telling me to fight hard; that we had too much left to do together. Usually not the emotional type, he was visibly shaken.

The doctor told him that if I didn't make a radical improvement within 48 hours, I most likely wouldn't make it. He said it might be best if the kids came – just in case.

Weeks later I was told that when they were talking to me, I kept saying I was tired, too tired. They also told me my youngest daughter kept begging me not to be too tired. It was just too much for them, though, and my husband had a friend take them home.

On the third day I finally woke up. Initially I had no recollection of anything that had happened since being brought to the ER by my husband. The nurse called him immediately to tell him I was awake and then began to recount the events of the last several days for me. I might not have believed her had I not been connected to so many different machines and wearing an oxygen mask as she explained what I had been through. It was a bit unnerving to say the least.

When the nurse removed the oxygen mask so I could speak, she wanted to know how I was feeling. All I could say was, 'tired'.

Tired; there was that word again. Five years later it still breaks my heart to think of my four beautiful children standing over my bed begging me to wake up, only to hear me say I was too tired for them. My son was in his early twenties and my daughters were nineteen, seventeen, and ten; they still needed me.

"Well, she said, I know some people who are going to be very happy to see you awake, so how would you like me to help you get a shower and a fresh gown on?"

Hearing her mention my family, I somehow remembered hearing Emma asking me to please not be too tired. I knew then I had to fight with all I had and not let her down.

"A shower? That would be lovely," I said.

I was able to be moved the next day to a regular room, but wasn't able to go home for two more weeks after that- and then with restrictions. My body had been through so much, it would never be the same.

I'm still 'plagued' with kidney problems and stones, but none have been as serious as that one. I just hope and pray my children never hear me say I'm too tired again.

> *"When you come to the end of your rope,*
> *tie a knot and hang on."*
> *~Franklin D. Roosevelt*

Perspective

Jodie Cox

Teens and parents, they're supposed to argue from time to time, right? It's just life. That's what I thought when I dropped off my daughter, Lacey, at the school to go on a field trip to an amusement park two hours away. She insisted on wearing a tank-top so she could get some sun. We both knew, that with her fair skin, the 'sun' she wanted to get would turn her skin lobster-red. It would be very painful.

Needless to say, we argued. She said she thought I treated her like a baby and I defended myself saying if she didn't want to be treated like one she shouldn't act like one. In the end, she got out of the car with me saying, 'don't come crying to me when you get sunburned'.

I hated the fact that we'd parted ways like that. If my kids don't know anything else, I don't want them to ever take a breath without knowing they are loved. No, our argument over a tank top didn't leave her feeling unloved, but, it was silly and unnecessary, and I decided to pick her up that evening with a hug and a bottle of sunburn relief lotion in hand. Unfortunately, though, it would only be less than an hour later that I would need a lot more than lotion to make Lacey feel better.

It's the phone call every parent dreads. Or in my case, two phone calls. The first was from Shelly, the mother of one of Lacey's friends who was also on the trip. Shelly's sister, who worked as an ER nurse at the local hospital, called and asked Shelly if Morgan was on a bus from the junior high. When she said yes, she was, Shelly was told that there had been an accident and that some of the kids, those with minor injuries, were being brought back there. Shelly asked if I'd heard anything. While she was still talking, my phone indicated I had a call coming in.

"Is this Mrs. Cox? Lacey Cox's mother?"

"Yes, who is this," I was trembling all over.

"This is Officer Delaney with the state police. The bus your daughter was riding on has been involved in an accident. I need you to come to Sullivan Regional Medical Center. I would advise you not to drive yourself. Can your husband or a friend bring you, or would you like an officer to pick you up?"

"Please," I tried to get the words out without sobbing, "please just tell me if she's alive."

"Mrs. Cox, we're not releasing any information on the condition of any of the children until we have everyone identified and families have been notified as to where to come. I'm sorry, but that's all I can tell you. Do you need a ride?"

"No, I'll call my husband. We'll be there as soon as possible."

I somehow made the call to Matthew, who came home immediately. A few minutes later, we were on our way to…we weren't sure. Matthew asked for details of the conversation I'd had with the police. How did he sound? Did he say anything else? I answered his questions, but other than that, I could say nothing. Or think of anything other than the fact that my last words to her were about me not being there for her, helping her. I knew Matthew wasn't asking to be accusatory or anything. He was just trying to process the situation in his own way. He was searching…grasping for anything to give hope. But all I could do is ask myself how I could be so stupid! How could I have let my precious daughter leave without telling her I loved her! It was then that I let the sobs that had been sitting in my throat escape. And they kept coming and coming and coming.

Matthew, unsure of what to do, kept asking if I was keeping something from him. Was Lacey dead and I just wasn't telling him? "No," I insisted. "It's not that." And then I told him about the argument we'd had over a stupid tank-top and sunburn.

Matthew, taking one hand off the steering wheel, touched my face and said we'd had the disagreement because I do love her and that Lacey knew that.

The state policeman I'd talked to on the phone had warned me that the traffic might be delayed, as they had to shut the Interstate down to clear the wreckage. Replaying those words sent waves of nausea rushing over me as the traffic slowed to a snail's pace and funneled into a single lane. I prayed desperately that the bus would no longer be there; I just didn't think Matthew or I (or the other parents, for that matter) should see the bus before we knew the condition of our children.

Trying to divert my attention, I pushed the 'on' button of the radio. It was set on a local station, which was giving a report on the accident… "reports of multiple injuries and at least three dead…" I switched it off, looked at Matthew and wiped the tears that were streaming down his face.

Mercifully, the authorities, knowing parents of the victims would be driving past the accident site, set up tarps to block the view of the wreck. One obstacle conquered...now on to the next.

Finally arriving at the hospital, we were taken to a room where other parents had gathered. Most, like Matthew and I, were shaken and anxious to know the condition of their children. We were given some details of the accident; a pick-up truck hauling a large piece of farm equipment on a trailer had a blow-out, lost control and the trailer had overturned directly in front of the bus. The bus subsequently hit the trailer head-on and was rear-ended by a semi. Considering the condition of the bus, it was a miracle 'it wasn't any worse than it was'.

We'd been there only a short while when four nurses came into the room and it was announced that, when your child's name was called, you were to go with the nurse who called their name.

Although we didn't know it until each group was in its own location, they'd divided us into groups based on the condition of each child. Lacey's name was called with eight others. Another group of four was called, followed by a group of nine and the final group had fifteen.

The largest group of children was those whose injuries consisted of bruises, cuts, and utter fear and anxiety. The group of nine had minor injuries; a broken ankle, two or three broken arms, concussions…injuries that needed attention, but were 'treat and release'. The eight that included our Lacey were the serious injuries, those that were either life-threatening or required immediate surgery or more acute care. And the four; Mallory, Leslie, John, and Rene weren't ever going to be going home again.

I'll never forget the anguished moans and cries we heard coming from behind those closed doors. Nor will I ever forget the stabbing guilt mixed with relief that I wasn't in there, too.

Lacey suffered a broken neck, head trauma, cuts, and bruises. We were told that as soon as we gave consent, they were prepared to operate on her neck as well as relieve the pressure on her brain. Before we could even ask, the doctor told us that time would tell if any permanent damage had been done.

Things will never be the same in our little town. School started a mere seven weeks after the incident-without the smiles and antics of several. Four precious lives would never pass through the doors again, and Lacey, along with three others, would require a home-bound tutor for the first few weeks of the school year.

Just before Thanksgiving break, Lacey went back to school walking on her own two feet. Thankful doesn't even begin to express how we feel for the chance we were given to remember to keep things in perspective and to remember that a tank top and sunburn aren't really such a big deal after all.

"As we express our gratitude, we must never forget that the highest appreciation is not to utter words, but to live by them."
~John Fitzgerald Kennedy

Uncommon Strength

Theresa Carpenter

I knew something was wrong; it would never have taken Jesse this long to gather up some extra wood. We were camping in a mountainous region of northern Arkansas. The weatherman had said the next three to four days was going to be virtually rain-free, but as we all know, they can be mistaken. So when we saw the clouds gathering, Jesse decided to gather a bit more wood and put it under our tarp to keep dry in case we needed it. Being six months pregnant, I stayed behind. After all, my growing belly wasn't much good for gathering wood.

How long had he been gone, though? I looked at my cell phone – it had been over an hour. We'd both grown up camping with our families and had taken extensive camping trips together, as well. Jesse knew what he was doing. But then anything could happen….

When another thirty minutes had passed, I decided I couldn't wait any longer to find out what, if anything, was wrong. What if Jesse was hurt and needed me? I kept telling myself, "Be smart about this. Don't take unnecessary risks that might hurt the baby. But find Jesse!"

The first thing I did was to gather up a couple bottles of water, a flash light, and the first-aid kit. Next I ripped up a t-shirt into strips to mark my way along whatever paths I took. Finally, I sent a text message to my dad telling him what was taking place. There wasn't much of a signal where we were, sketchy at best, but a text would come closer to going through than a call.

"Okay, Tessa," I told myself. "You can do this. Jesse's always been there for you. It's your turn."

I started off in the direction he'd gone. It was pretty easy to follow his tracks for the first ten minutes or so. It was obvious he'd piled a bit of wood here and there to gather on his way back. Smart thinking; why carry it as you gathered, right?

But then something changed. The underbrush was flattened everywhere – not just in steps. And this new 'path' seemed to stop at the rocks. Why would Jesse go to the rocks to find wood?

For lack of any better idea, I started picking my way carefully across the rocky area toward a rocky hillside with deep clefts cut into it, so deep they were really more like little caves. I'd taken just a couple of steps when I saw the blood.

Getting down to take a closer look, it didn't take an expert to know it was fresh. My eyes immediately started scanning in all directions for more. Of course, there'd be more. Nothing bleeds just one drop of blood out in the woods. There was another...and another... and another.... As my walk began to be more of a climb, I started to worry about falling; hurting myself, our baby and making myself useless to Jesse. But I knew I had to find him. Who else would be bleeding in these woods? This was his blood and he needed me.

I wanted to panic, but somehow held myself in check. "Tessa, keep it together," I kept telling myself. "It's not going to do anyone any good if you lose it." The other 'side' of me wanted to argue with that reasoning, but thankfully didn't win out. And just seconds later, I'd know what a blessing that was.

"Tessa...Tessa...over here!"
That was Jesse. I started looking, searching for where the voice had come from. And why was it barely above a whisper?

"Tessa, Look slowly to your right. Don't make any sudden moves!"

I spotted Jesse wedged between some large rocks in one of the clefts of the hill. What was he doing...and then I heard the moaning growl that answered my question. A momma bear with two cubs came from behind another large rock, the momma carrying the remains of something in her jaws. The bear hadn't yet seen me, but I saw her nose hit the air. She knew I was there.

"Tessa," Jesse whispered, "walk toward me, slowly and without taking your eyes off that bear. Slow, honey, slow and easy."

I had to fight with everything in me to not run to Jesse, but I knew he was right. So I took a step backwards. I kept stepping slowly and carefully until I felt Jesse's hand take mine and guide me into the space behind the rocks he was wedged between.

The blood was his; he'd gouged his shin on the rocks when he was getting away from the protective mother bear. He told me he'd come up on them while she was tearing into the deer and feeding her cubs. He'd surprised them and she wasn't happy about it. His plan was to wait her out before heading back to camp.

For the next couple of hours Jesse and I sipped the water I'd brought and stayed as quiet as we could. The bear and her cubs had decided the rocks warmed by the sunshine was the perfect place for a nap; making it impossible for us to get away. When naptime was over, though, they lazily stretched, sniffed the air, and started to walk away toward the lake.

Waiting what we thought was a safe amount of time, Jesse and I didn't dawdle getting out of the rocks to head to camp. The rain we thought was coming, the reason Jesse had left camp in the first place, started to fall. Hurrying as fast as my belly would let me, we made our way back through the woods; Jesse complimenting me for keeping such a clear head every time we'd pass one of my flags.

We were just within sight of camp when we heard the commotion. The bears had made their way to our camp and were ransacking the cooler and other groceries I'd set out on the table. And then they stopped. The momma bear turned her head toward us, sniffed, and started in our direction. Jesse and I both knew I was not going to be able to outrun the bear. And we were running out of time. She'd spied us and wasn't happy for the 'intrusion'. Jesse, acting on instinct, picked up a fallen log-much larger than he'd normally pick up. As the bear ran at us, Jesse yelled at me to run for the car and he swung the log with all his might like he would have swung a bat on the softball field.

Jesse's not what you'd call wiry, but he's not into pumping iron, either. But in that moment, when protecting his wife and child meant life or death for us all. Jesse was able to find uncommon strength to land the swing across the bear's head. It knocked her down and dazed her just long enough for both of us to make it to the car. We knew there was a chance the bear would attempt to have her revenge, but fortunately, her cubs had joined her and still dazed, they decided to leave.

I'd had the forethought to put the car keys in the first-aid kit that was still on my back, so leaving everything else behind, Jesse put the keys in the ignition and we drove away.

We still love camping and go with our three children. But we are more aware than the average camper that anything can happen at any time and the preparedness and respect for the natural residents of the forest should take top priority when enjoying the great outdoors.

"There is only one thing more painful than learning from experience, and that is not learning from experience."
~Laurence J. Peter

Three Year Homecoming

Linda Davis

When I think about the last eight years of my life, I see-saw back and forth between wondering how in the world I could have been so naïve and foolish to have ever thought my ex-husband was ever worthy of my love and remembering the time we were in love and being thankful for the children that love gave me.

But loving my children isn't something I've been able to do in the conventional way most mothers enjoy.

Ron and I met in college and married the summer before he entered medical school. I'd graduated with a degree in history and got a job teaching elementary level social studies. I loved it. Lesson plans and grading filled the time that Ron was working and studying. My dad is a doctor so I understood the long hours and didn't complain. We were happy and looking forward to the day when life would become more normal and we could start our family.

The week after his graduation from medical school, I found out we were expecting our son. Two years later, our daughter was born. Everything was just as we'd planned and hoped for it to be.

The first sign of trouble was at our son's eighth birthday party, though. Among the guests was the son of one of the nurses in Ron's office. The little boy wasn't the problem, his mother was. It was obvious that she and Ron were unduly comfortable with one another. It was both embarrassing and hurtful.

A couple of months passed and it seemed as if he was just daring me to ask him about their relationship. When I did, he admitted they'd been sleeping together for several months and that they had every intention of being together. She'd already left her husband. I was understandably angry and hurt. After all we'd accomplished together and this is what I got.

Things began to get messy. Ron's girlfriend, 'Leah', decided she wanted my home. When I refused to even consider such a thing, she started spreading rumors about me being unstable. She and Ron began to talk to the kids – MY kids-about my mental health.

At the advice of my lawyer, I got a temporary order keeping Ron's girlfriend from being around my children. He was furious and said I'd pay for keeping him from moving on with his life.

It was a Wednesday. I went to pick up the kids from school but they didn't come out like they normally did. When it was clear everyone was out that was coming, I parked and went in. My daughter's teacher was coming out of her classroom so I stopped and asked her where my daughter was.

"Your husband, uh, I mean the kids' father picked them up today. He checked them out about a half hour before the bell rang. He said you'd sent him.... Did we do something wrong?"

I turned and ran from the building and drove straight to the police station. This was before everyone had a cell phone, so when I got there I tried calling Ron but naturally got no answer. I called my parents, my lawyer, and Ron's office. The receptionist at the office told me 'Leah' had quit yesterday and that Ron had said he was taking a vacation-to cancel his appointments for a couple of weeks. My children were gone! My ex-husband had stolen my children!

The police filed all the necessary paperwork, but because no custody agreement had been reached and filed with the court, he still had as much right to the children as I had.

We went to Ron's apartment, which had basically been cleared out and no hint of where he was going could be found. Later on I learned from a neighbor that Ron had brought the kids to our house (he knew where the key was) and took some of their things as well. He intended to be gone a while.

I was hysterical. Inconsolable is more like it. Where were my babies? Who was this man I'd married? The man I married would never have done this to me! And I was completely at his mercy.

Hours turned to days and days to weeks. No sign of Ron or the kids. 'Leah' was gone, having left her son with his father. Were my children with that woman? What was she telling them about why I wasn't with them?

Three weeks after he'd taken off, Ron called. The kids were crying and missed me, so he let me talk to them for just a short while. I assured them that I loved them, that I did not want them to be away from me, and that I would do everything I could to bring them home. I was able to get them to tell me that they were in an airport, but didn't know where. My daughter said they were going somewhere where their dad could be a doctor. I barely got to tell them I loved them again before I heard 'Leah' say it was time to go. Click.

I'd never taken advantage of the fact that my family was wealthy. I'd not been the type of kid to want all the latest and most expensive clothes and such. But when Dad and Mom offered funds to hire a private detective to find my children, I accepted in a heartbeat.

He traced them to the airport in Dallas, an international flight. But from there he could find nothing. Weekly reports came in, for a few months, but then trickled to monthly.

Birthdays and holidays were excruciating. I'd console myself with looking at their pictures, buying gifts I thought they'd like and tried to picture them in my mind as they were changing and growing without me.

The months ticked by and in spite of everything, I had to continue to live life. My life revolved around looking for my children and teaching. I had no social life; my only friends were the police, the detective, and my parents. I can't say time flew by, because it didn't. Each day dragged by. But when three years had passed, I was beginning to think I'd never see my children again.

But three years and sixteen days after Ron had walked out of the school with my children, I got a call from the detective. 'Leah' had re-entered the country from Panama. And according to her passport, Panama had been her destination three years previously. I was elated and scared. Were they in Panama? Would they want to see me? What if they'd been poisoned against me? What if they didn't remember me?

'Leah' checked into a hotel in Dallas and spent the next few days searching for a job. The detective flew down there and along with the police, questioned her. It took very little effort (love scorned, you know) to learn that she and Ron had taken the kids to Panama from the get-go. But all of Ron's promises had been nothing but that – promises – and she'd gotten fed up and left a year later. She'd married a Panamanian, but he'd left her for a younger woman (fair is fair), so she'd come back to the States to try to get her life back together.

I took the first plane to Panama I could get. Yes, it was a bit premature, but you tell me what you'd do? The detective joined me the following day to meet with the Panamanian officials. Three days later Ron was arrested for being in the country illegally and my children were in my arms.

Their homecoming wasn't without awkwardness and stressful moments. I had to be careful to not treat them as if they were still six and eight. But with counseling and lots of love, we've made it.

That was three years ago. Ron was recently released from prison. His lawyer contacted me; asking me if I would allow supervised visits between him and the kids. My first inclination was a resounding NO! But when I remembered the way I felt each day thinking I might never see them again, I just didn't have it in me to do so. Instead, I told him I'd leave it up to the kids. And when they're ready, I'll not stand in their way.

> "We have two lives - the one we learn with
> and the life we live after that."
> ~Bernard Malamud, The Natural

The Cost of Choosing

Valerie Mayville

Lonnie, our children, our infant granddaughter, and I set off to see America. Well, part of it, any way. We hadn't taken a road trip in the 'ole RV' for three or four years. In fact, we'd decided to sell it, but wanted to make a few more memories before we did. That RV had taken our family to the Grand Canyon, Disney World, and Washington DC in the years we'd owned it and for its final voyage, we were heading to Washington and Oregon. We'd never been there, and we wanted to take advantage of being able to spend time on the ski slopes and the ocean without traveling more than a couple of hours.

We were having a wonderful time; stopping along the way whenever we saw something we thought would be fun. Baby Camille, only six weeks old, was exceeding our expectations for sleeping at night. In close quarters, that could have been an issue, but it wasn't. Yes, this would be yet another Austin family memory-maker.

We were headed to Seattle to take in the sights. Other than a bit of sunburn, everyone was feeling great and ready to make the most of this last leg of the trip. As we were driving along the curvy mountain roads, though, Lonnie noticed the brakes were grabbing a bit. He said he didn't think it was anything to worry about, but that we'd stop at the first gas station so he could check things over just to be sure. I could tell he was becoming more and more concerned about the situation as we continued to make our way down the mountain and that there was indeed something wrong with the brakes on the RV.

"Did that sign say three miles," Lonnie asked. "I hope it's a short three miles because I don't think these brakes have much left in them."

He'd no more gotten the words out of his mouth than we rounded the curve to make the final descent off the mountain. But our relief quickly faded when we realized the descent was a ten percent grade and not without curves. Lonnie knew we were in trouble and asked everyone to please listen to him. He said the brakes were all but gone on the RV and that he didn't see how we could possibly make it to the bottom without wrecking. He asked that everyone gather in the center of the vehicle and pad ourselves with pillows and blankets. He apologized for what he felt sure was going to happen; he prayed and then told us all how much he loved us.

Putting the RV in neutral, he began to carefully maneuver us toward town. Thankfully there was no traffic in front of us, but we were beginning to gather speed. We were almost to the bottom, and though scared and shaken, still in one piece.

"Please, Lord," I prayed. "Please don't take my children." Just ahead was a scenic view and picnic area. The cement block restrooms would provide the perfect stop for us rather than risking hurting someone in town. But it was filled with people. Lonnie said there was no way he was going to endanger the lives of others. That's when he made the choice – the only choice he had to make. He had to steer past the rest stop and crash the RV into the massive piles of rock on the other side of it.

"Thank you, Val, for loving me and making me happy." Those were the last words Lonnie said to me.

The police officer said he'd died instantly – that he hadn't suffered. But that was little consolation for my family and me. Thankfully Camille was unharmed, not so much as a scratch. I had a broken leg, my son and daughter-in-law, Camille's parents, both had broken ribs and cuts and my daughter had a concussion, broken ribs and a partially collapsed lung. My youngest son, however, suffered internal injuries, both legs were broken, and he had swelling around the brain.

I didn't know which way to turn, what to do, where to go. I couldn't take a deep breath much less think straight. I watched my son, Bryce, become his father; taking charge gently, but firmly, calling family back home to tell them what had happened and to make arrangements for our journey home; bringing comfort to his wife, to me and to his younger siblings.

The community was wonderful. They took those of us who didn't have to remain in the hospital into their homes to care for us, feed us, clothe us, and let us know we were not alone even though we were so far from home. A near-by car rental agency donated a van to take us home and the local funeral home donated their services.

The police and media all had questions for us. It was obvious to the policemen responsible for reconstructing the accident that Lonnie could have taken the less severe way out and hit the building. I heard them talking to each other about it – saying it was too bad he hadn't thought about doing that. "But," one said to the other, "maybe he did think about it."

"Oh, yes," I said, "he thought about it alright. But there were people all around – families just like ours. He said he didn't have the right or the heart to put them in danger."

"It's too bad," one of them said, "if he had of, he would most likely still be alive."

Now don't get me wrong, my heart was aching for my Lonnie – it still does. I couldn't even begin to imagine how I was going to go home without him, but I did know one thing.

"No, he did the right thing – he chose to die so innocent people wouldn't have to."

"But he was innocent, too. It wasn't his fault the brakes went out."

"I know," I replied, "but Lonnie lived to show others who Jesus is and putting others before himself is – was – like breathing to him."

As a Christian, I'd always talked the talk about there being a reason for everything and something good coming from everything. Lonnie and I had taught our children to do the same. But now, well now we had to walk the walk, so to speak.

So walk we did. Functioning only by the grace of God, we pulled together as a family to grieve together, heal together, and keep watch over Keaton as he healed. Thankfully the swelling of his brain diminished within three or four days with nothing more than short-term memory loss (a blessing, to be sure). The internal injuries were less serious than first thought; a tear in the spleen that required surgery. His legs were both casted; more of a hassle for him than anything after the swelling and initial pain subsided.

Keaton's progress surpassed the doctors' expectations, allowing him to be released from the hospital eight days after the accident. By then, we'd all become quite close to our host families and had been touched by their love and generosity. But we were also ready to be home with family and friends who would be able to love us through our grief and understand the hole in our hearts.

The day before we left for home, the newspaper reporter who'd talked to me on the day of the accident asked if he could take the family to lunch. As we were all seated around the table, he said he had one question he'd like each of us to answer, "How? How had we been able to smile through our tears?"

Our answer: we had a choice-just like Lonnie had a choice. And also like Lonnie, we did what we knew in our hearts to be the right thing.

That was eight years ago. Lonnie's absence still tugs at my heart, especially when another child marries or a grandchild is born; on birthdays, our anniversary, and when the simplest things make his absence seem almost unbearable. But then I think of all he gave to our family and how the choice he made that day undoubtedly gave life and love to others.

"Courage is not the absence of fear, but rather the judgment that something else is more important than fear." ~Ambrose Redmoon

Healing the Grief

Friends to the End

Nate Mailey

It was the Saturday before Mother's Day, 2008. We'd spent the day planting flowers, raking the yard, and enjoying the kids and grandkids home for the weekend. Yep, all in all, it had been a great day.

It looked like we'd gotten done just in time, though. The sky took on the Spring storm look. And with a houseful of grandkids, I wasn't willing to take any chances in case of a tornado. So while my wife and daughters started working on dinner, I turned on the television to see if they were giving any weather warnings. Having lived in Southwest Missouri all seventy-seven years of my life, I've been through more tornado watches and warnings than I could ever possibly count. I'd even seen a few small tornados touch down, but even I wasn't prepared for what they were saying.

"A large funnel has been spotted and is on the ground in the Spring City area, traveling south. The path the tornado is expected to take will encompass the people living along highways 42 and 86. People in this area need to take cover immediately...."

"Come on, to the basement...NOW!" I nearly shouted. "Get the kids and go now!"

The weather alerts going off had gotten everyone's attention and in just a few seconds, everyone was heading for the basement. I took up the rear, taking the time to open a few windows, grab a flashlight and my cell phone. This didn't take more than two, three minutes at the most, but by the time I reached the basement door to head downstairs, the rain had stopped, the sky was green and the air perfectly still. Some would call it intuition, others would call it premonition, but I knew in my heart that something bad was about to happen. I felt like someone was calling for help and I couldn't get to them in time.

The others had turned on the television in the rec room and were listening as the weather man was relaying the information that the tornado was still on the ground, showing no mercy to anything in its path. All the while, we could hear the wind roaring like never before. And then it was over. It seemed like hours, but just like you hear from other survivors of storms like this, it was actually a couple of minutes, tops. Then the rain started in again with a vengeance.

I surveyed the damage from the front and back porch. Only a couple of trees down, flower pots strewn everywhere and a small portion of the roof from one of the outbuildings ripped off. Nothing not easily repaired. Was the weather man wrong? He'd said the brunt of the storm had hit the communities of Racine and Seneca. We were less than a mile from 86 Highway and Racine. We'd had worse. And then the phone rang.

Paul and Deanne had been among our closest friends for more than fifty years. Deanne was on the other end of the line. She said the tornado had in fact come down highway 86, that their house along with everyone else's as far as she could see was gone – and that she couldn't find Paul.

We didn't live much more than a mile from them! How could that be? After telling her I was on my way, I gave the phone to my wife so she could comfort and encourage Deanne. I drove the short distance from the house to the highway, noticing our neighbors had sustained about the same amount of damage we had. But when I turned onto the highway, it was as if I'd entered another world. Trees, houses, and barns were leveled. Cars and trucks and dead cattle were scattered around like a discarded newspaper. I couldn't believe what I was seeing.

I found Deanne sitting on a pile of rubble that had been her kitchen, crying. She didn't want to leave without knowing where Paul was, but it was pouring down rain and lightening was all around. I assured her I would come right back after I took her to our house where she'd be safe and dry and have our family to be with.

The homes of other friends had also been destroyed. I counted nine in the short distance traveled between our two homes. The calls had already started coming in – every house along a six mile section of a county road was leveled, several people hurt, dozens of cattle killed or missing, chicken and turkey houses collapsed killing hundreds of animals. The town of Seneca hadn't fared any better. Three people were missing, businesses and houses destroyed and some minor injuries.

When I got back to Paul and Deanne's, I wasn't sure where to start looking. What had happened to my friend? Deanne said he'd been right behind her on the stairs leading to the basement. She said they saw the funnel cloud coming and were going to the basement when there was a loud sucking sound and the house was gone.

I looked for almost an hour before I found him. He was quite a distance from the house-obviously carried by the force of the tornado. He'd most likely died quickly and without suffering.

I called 911, but when I told them he was deceased, they said that unfortunately, it would be several hours before they could get there – injuries had to take priority. Since the closest hospital was almost twenty miles away, I knew it would be a while. The next call was to Deanne. How do you give someone news like that over the phone? She'd known in her heart Paul hadn't survived the storm, but losing her partner of more than fifty years was devastating in any circumstance. Hearing that it would be morning before anyone could get to him was even more worrisome. How could she just leave him there? I assured her he wouldn't be alone.

Paul had been there for me when both my mother and father had passed away and when we'd lost our prematurely born grandson. We'd gone on family camping trips together, worshipped together, worked in the hay field together and helped one another build the houses we lived in. I wasn't going to desert him now – not when he needed me most.

So after finding something to cover him with, to keep him dry, I sat down beside him to wait and say goodbye to one of the finest men I'd ever known.

Around two or three that next morning I heard a couple of young men approaching. They were obviously up to no good; talking about what they'd found here and there and the ground they wanted to cover before daylight. Looters!

I'm not sure what was worse, finding my long time friend lying in the rubble of what had been his home or hearing the disgusting conversation of these hoodlums.

I knew they hadn't seen me yet, but I wanted them to know I was there. I hoped my being there would stop their hideous behavior. I shined my light on them and asked them who they were and had they come to help me take Paul's body to the funeral home. They said they were assessing the damage done and collecting items for home owners. They'd obviously rehearsed their excuse, but they sounded less than confident when it sunk in that I'd mentioned the words funeral home. Even in the dark with only a flashlight to see by, I could tell they were nervous.

I remember being so relieved that they were nervous, because the two of them — even one of them — could have taken me if any physical confrontation had taken place. But not wanting them to sense anything other than the fact I was in control of the situation, I told them there wasn't anything needing to be done here, that the funeral home was on its way, and that they needed to go on their way. They hesitated, whispered to one another, and took a few steps toward me. Were they even lower than I thought? Without really even thinking, I stood up and repeated myself in what the kids always called my 'I mean business so don't mess with me' voice, adding that they needed to be respectful of the dead.

They shrugged their shoulders, whispered to one another again and then turned around and walked away. I'm not embarrassed to admit I'd never been more relieved about anything in my life, but I couldn't' help wondering if they'd be back. Needless to say that I didn't close my eyes the rest of the night, but instead, kept vigil over Paul and what little was salvageable of his and Deanne's belongings. I thought about a lot of things that night, but any time my mind came back to those two guys, I'd cringe at the thought of what would have happened had I not been there to watch over Paul.

The rain stopped at some point. And as the sun began to come up I remember hearing the birds start to sing and call out to one another. The tree tops were now on the ground, but they were there, so the birds still had a place to land. I remember thinking as I looked out at the scattered debris thinking that these folks should be as fortunate as the birds. But it would take a lot more to provide them a safe place to land.

A short time later the EMT's arrived to remove Paul's body. They commented on my staying with him, asked me why I'd done it. "He's my friend," I said. "And he would have done the same for me."

"Be true to your work, your word, and your friend."
~Henry David Thoreau

3 A.M.

Logan Preston

Heavy rain hammered down from the sky that night, as if the moon had been spinning around in its silent grave, a ferocious fury of water splattering at my feet as I stood at the edge of the JFK train bridge. For weeks now, the image of shattered limbs cutting through the damp March atmosphere had been leaving skid marks on my mind, an innocent man thrust into the unforgiving jaws of a busy city intersection by the force of a reckless Impala driver. While the scene was most assuredly an accident, the driver's sudden speeding away certainly wasn't, his anxious foot becoming much more focused as he drove high hell into the gas pedal, maneuvering around the crippled pile of bone and flesh heaped on the asphalt. Throughout the entire scene, I had been standing motionless with my bicycle straddled between my legs, a grape-scented lollipop hanging loose from my jaw as the tragedy unfolded before me, fingers coiling around my rubber handlebars like a viper as I was shaken to my depths by what I had just witnessed.

Ever since this incident had occurred, I had been feeling a deep anxiety about going anywhere near densely populated streets. Knowing that bicyclists were even more at risk for accidents than pedestrians, I had retired my two-wheeled demon into the closet of my living room, my skin crawling every time I remembered the way the handlebars' rubber burned into my palms. Although I was normally a very attentive student, focusing in class had become incredibly difficult, my brain unable to shake what had transpired. It was getting to the point where I found myself staying up late in the evening, in a mad attempt to ward off sleep, trying to avoid the thought of reckless death stampeding across my synapses.

In addition to the heart wrenching image that had been burned into my memory, I also felt wildly restless over just how little I did to help. I didn't go over to the man to see if he was okay, I didn't even call 911, if only because I assumed someone else would have by then. In a sense, I couldn't help but feel I wasn't any better than the man who had committed this heinous crime. Sure, I hadn't actually injured anyone, but not to try and do something about this sad wreck of a human being only filled me with tremendous guilt upon turning on the evening news, and learning that he had failed to survive his injuries.

This evening though, I had found the anxiety to be too much to deal with. I had been avoiding the outside world so much during the last fortnight, fearing the thought of running into someone as coldhearted as the man who murdered that helpless soul in a cold frenzy. Still, I knew my condition would only worsen if I didn't try to do something about it.

Looking over to my alarm clock, I realized that it was now the middle of the night: 3 AM, to be precise. Even in as hectic a city as this, there was almost no one out at such a low hour, a common breaking point for even the most restless of insomniacs. Although I could hear a symphony of heavy rain tattering against my window pane, I decided I had no choice but to snatch my midnight blue umbrella from its holster, and slip out of the house into the cold, relentless night.

Although I was clear and direct in my objective of getting outside, my idea of where I was actually headed was a complete mystery to me. All I knew was that I had to simply keep walking, my boot encased feet traversing the gravelly hill with a great frenzy. I decided that if there was any way I would get over my fear of city streets, not to mention my recurring shame, I would have to revisit that intersection where the incident had taken place so long ago. Realizing I had no direction in mind other than straight ahead, I pressed onwards towards Schuylkill Trailway, its namesake taken from the majestic river which bordered this newly paved path. I made sure to huddle close to my umbrella's cold, sleek handle as I was carried down this sloping corridor, the moon's faint reflection rippling in the river's waters. To avoid any further sadness, I decided to keep my head pointed toward the ground, not wanting to stare at any of the homeless people taking refuge underneath the various bridges crossing the path. However, this frantic yet confident stride was swiftly broken as I heard what sounded like a blaring car horn in the distance, causing me to lose all composure, and break into a heated dash towards the end of the path, each foot soaring in front of the other, allowing the rain to catch the cuffs of my jeans as I bounded up the stairs to Market Street.

I could feel my mental state deteriorating quickly, thoughts of grief bounding into the forefront of my head as my eyes scanned the cityscape. I could feel a few tears leaking from my ducts, mixing with the rainwater on the pavement below as they dripped from my face. I was in no condition to revisit that block. In fact, I could only imagine my tears becoming more abundant the closer I got to that crime scene, my hands shaking, both from my fear and the stagnant chill ripping through the air. However, I knew I couldn't just waste my journey out into the damp night. Instead, I resolved to change my destination to the John F Kennedy train bridge I had passed under on my way here.

Ever since I was a little kid, I had observed that there was a strange dirt hill leading up from the street to this pebble infused passageway, a flurry of suburban rail liners chugging along its majesty every single day. Although it was a struggle to ascend such a hill, the slippery rocks buried in the dirt nearly caused me to lose my footing, I managed to ascend my way to the top of the bridge without much struggle. Although the bridge was meant for trains, it was bordered by two conveniently sized walkways, as if I was meant to come up here myself.

Upon reaching the top of the bridge, I found myself taking a firm stance atop the 22nd Street overpass. I pondered for a moment the concept of leaping off this 20 foot high-rise and plummeting to my death below as thunder crackled above my head, sending shockwaves through the silent night. I couldn't help but consider how I wasn't much better than that driver for my lack of action.

However, when the thought of suicide crossed my mind, a further sinking feeling isn't what overcame me. Instead, I started to feel anger. I felt pure, seething rage coursing through my fists – rage that I would even so much consider self-harm as a just reaction.

To kill myself would be an insult to the memory of the man I had the unfortunate circumstance of watching as he was forced to his untimely death. Instead, I realized I needed to do the opposite. Although there was no way I could simply take back my lack of compassion during that blood drenched scene, I knew I could make it right through the help of others. Although I wasn't sure at that moment just how exactly that positivity would express itself, I knew then that if there was any one thing you could regret in your life, it was not having done a single thing. And that was not a regret I wanted slashed into my conscience.

I had stopped shivering and my head lifted from its solemn bow. I took a deep breath into my chest and began climbing down from the bridge, into a more fulfilling, more positive existence.

"Rock bottom is good solid ground, and a dead end street is just a place to turn around."
~Buddy Buie and J.R. Cobb, "Rock Bottom" (song)

Nellie

Olivia Strong

For as long as I can remember, there have been old people in my life. My great-grandmother lived in a little house on our farm. There were several elderly people at our church I was with each Sunday and Wednesday, and the couple that lived across the road from us was like another set of grandparents to my brother, sisters, and me. That's why it was only natural when, as 7th grade student council president, I signed up for the 'Bridging the Generation Gap' project to fulfill my community service expectation.

Every other week, I'd spend an hour after school visiting the nursing home, handing out mail, filling water glasses, and just being a friendly face for the residents. That's how I met Nellie.

Nellie was short and a little on the chubby side. She had thick white hair that she kept in a bun on the top of her head, and she always wore a pearl necklace. It had been a gift from her husband on their wedding day. They'd raised seven children and been married for fifty-five years before he died several years previous.

Most of her children lived far away, but those who didn't came to see her regularly. So it wasn't that Nellie didn't have anyone, but there was just something about her that made me love her. It wasn't long before I was getting done as quickly as possible with my other duties to spend as much time as possible with Nellie. My mom even took me to see her once a week after school while my older sister was at piano lessons.

Nellie told me stories about herself and her children, she'd quiz me to see if I knew my spelling words and we'd read Nancy Drew books together. Her daughters had loved them and so did I.

When the end of the school year came, I was worried I wouldn't get to see Nellie any more. But thankfully, my mom and dad were both delighted and proud of my love for Nellie and continued to take me to see her each week. The only times I missed were when I was at church camp, our family camping trip and when I had the flu. On Nellie's birthday, we took her ice cream and for each holiday, a card and little gift or basket of goodies.

That's how it was for two years. But then as all teenagers do, I got busy. My dance classes went from once a week to three times a week, and my visits with Nellie went from once a week to once a month.

Christmas was a few weeks away and my mom was taking the junior high and high school youth group to the homes of the elderly people in our church to sing carols and to give them cookies and other Christmas goodies. A few of the people lived in an assisted living facility directly across the street from the nursing home where Nellie lived, so I asked my mom if she'd drop me off there while the rest of them went elsewhere. She agreed, saying we'd all come in and sing to Nellie when she picked me up. So with a plate of cookies in one hand, a card and gift in the other, I hurried through the doors of the nursing home and headed straight for Nellie's room.

When my mom and the other kids came to pick me up, I was sitting on the bench in front of the nursing home crying my eyes out. Nellie had passed away less than two weeks prior to my visit. She'd died in her sleep-peacefully and without sickness or pain. Her big, beautiful heart had simply stopped beating.

The nurses said they'd tried to remember my last name, but couldn't, and were very sorry they'd not been able to get a hold of me. I said 'thank you', that I appreciated their concern, but it really didn't matter. Nellie was gone and I hadn't even said good-bye.

There was little anyone could say or do to make me feel less guilty about letting life get in the way of going to see her as often as I had in the past. But a week later, when I received a little package in the mail, my heart was made a bit lighter.

"Dear Olivia,

We want you to know how grateful we are for your friendship to our mother, Nellie Shide. She was always telling us what a beautiful young lady you are – inside and out – and how much she looked forward to your visits. It's rare these days to find someone such as yourself who would take the time to befriend someone so different from yourself. We thank you and want you to know that she loved you very much. We are enclosing the pictures of the two of you together and her Bible. We hope they will bring you fond memories of our mother.

Sincerely,

The children of Nellie Shide"

I'll remember her always, love her forever and look forward to seeing her again some day.

"No one ever really dies as long as they took the time to leave us with fond memories."

~Chris Sorensen

When Terrorism Wasn't a Word

Agathe Girard

Before we'd started sending our boys off to help with the war, nobody worked on Sunday. But with the war on overseas, that had changed for a lot of people.

My husband, Pete, and one of my older brothers, Olaf, had both been hired to work on the road crew that was building what is known as Rt. 66 in our area. They were blasting through the rock to make way for the road, and for whatever reason, they were doing it on Sunday. What was even more unusual was that we were having unseasonably warm weather in the Ozarks that December; sunny and not too terribly, cold. They were comfortable working with nothing more than a light jacket over their work clothes.

In fact, it was so nice that my sisters and I decided, after church, we'd all get together for dinner at my house. One of my sisters and her husband were moving out to California soon and we wanted to all be together, knowing we wouldn't have many opportunities like this again. Besides, the kids could all play outside. So after church that day, my parents, me, my three children, my five sisters and their spouses, one brother and his wife, and about twenty nieces and nephews spent the afternoon enjoying good food and the joys of being together.

Some had cameras with them, so we decided to go outside and take a few pictures. My five sisters and I were lined up and we'd just snapped a picture of 'us girls' when Pete and Olaf pulled up in Olaf's truck. It was too early for them to be done for the day, even on Sunday, and we knew by the look on their faces that something was wrong.

"What's wrong," I asked Pete.

"Haven't you heard? The Japs bombed our ships in a place called Pearl Harbor over in Hawaii. We lost a lot of boys. It's really bad. They sent us all home 'cause they said we need to be listening to the radio to see if they start attacking other places."

We were shocked, but somehow we crowded into our little sitting room. With four chairs, a small table, a couple of lamps and a radio, it was tight, but no one made a sound as we listened to the continued news reports coming in. An occasional gasp or grunt was detectable over something we'd hear, but other than that, we were just all too shocked and upset to say much of anything. After hearing that the President would be speaking to the country the next day, we turned the radio off and began trying to figure things out in our own minds. Why? What did the Japanese want? We had all sorts of questions, but no answers.

The next day, Pete and I listened to President Roosevelt's speech. I remember thinking it sure must be hard to be him at a time like this. He used the words 'deliberate' and 'hostile'. He said our country – our way of life – was in 'grave danger'. He went on to say that he was certain, however, that we would see victory and that we would, "triumph…so help us, God."

Never once did he say the words 'terrorism' or 'terrorist'. I don't know if anyone would have known what he meant if he had. Besides, it really doesn't matter what you call it, it was still just mean and black-hearted, plain and simple.

Well, after that, most every man and boy in the county was called up for the draft, Pete included. I fretted all that afternoon while he was at the draft board getting his physical. I wondered where he'd go. For how long? What if he got hurt or worse? In lots of ways, I think we got the 'worse'.

When Pete got home, he sat me down and told me he wouldn't be going off to the war, but that he would be leaving. Turns out he had TB. See, his dad had died of it when Pete was only seven. If he'd had it all that time nobody really knows. But what they did know was that he had it now and that it wasn't safe for him to be with us.

Over the next two years, while Pete was away at the sanatorium-a hospital for people with TB – I learned what 'terror' was; even though I didn't call it that.

I had three small children under the age of seven and no way to provide for us other than our farm. I didn't know how I'd make it. If it hadn't been for the food I'd canned from the garden and for my uncle, who owned the local store, leaving 'anonymous' gifts now and then, I don't think I would have survived.

Pete eventually got well and got to come home. But he wasn't strong enough to farm. Eventually we sold the farm to his brother and moved to town. We went on to have a good life together before he died almost thirty years ago.

You didn't have to be in Pearl Harbor that day for it to change your life. It changed us all. Were we scared? Yes, we were. But we didn't give the enemy the name 'terrorist'. We just called it like it was, and fought until we'd gotten the victory Roosevelt said we had it in us to get.

"Count the garden by the flowers, never by the leaves that fall. Count your life with smiles and not the tears that roll." ~Author Unknown

They Acted as if Everything was Fine
Olivia Middleton

I sat in the front seat of the car waiting for my husband to purchase diapers for our daughter, who was nearly two. I was still numb from the events of the last three days and wondered how the people walking in and out of the store could be so uncaring. They were acting as if everything was fine. But it wasn't fine – I'd just buried my son! How could they be so uncaring?

Keith and I were excited when we found out I was expecting again. Yes, it would be a challenge having two little ones so close in age, but Dena was a joy. It would be fine. I was also thrilled not to be as sick with this baby as I had been with Dena. Morning sickness? You mean all-day sickness!

Our insurance was very basic, it didn't cover the 'extras' like sonograms unless deemed necessary. But when I was six months along, the doctor ordered one because he was concerned I wasn't measuring what I should in regards to the baby's growth. I wasn't too concerned in the beginning, but it wasn't long before I could see the looks of concern and sadness on the faces of the nurse technician. One of them immediately went for the doctor.

My baby, a boy, had not developed properly. His brain had not developed beyond the stem. They called it anencephaly. He had no brain or skull past the forehead, only soft tissue. I was reeling. I'd come for my regular appointment. Why were they telling me this? I needed my daughter. Where had the nurse taken her? I needed my husband. Would I be able to get a hold of him? He was working in the fields at his mom and dad's farm, and this was before cell phone days.

The nurses must have read my mind. The one who'd offered to watch Dena while I was getting the ultrasound done, brought her to me. I couldn't hold her close enough. They also asked me how to contact Keith. The doctor wanted to see us together and did not want me leaving the office without someone.

Keith had come home to get some tools and answered the phone. He immediately came to the doctor's office to hear the news. After giving us the statistics and cold hard facts about our son not surviving for more than an hour or so when he was delivered, he went on to say there was no reason to put ourselves through that, so he'd set up an induced delivery as soon as possible. Did we want it this week?

Numb, we asked to be left alone for a few minutes. Thankfully we were able to pull it together enough to recognize what the doctor was saying. He wanted us to terminate the pregnancy immediately. He was asking us to give up our son sooner rather than later.

We couldn't. It wasn't even an option as far as we were concerned. No, we weren't expecting a re-take on the sonogram to reveal a tragic error had been made, but we did know that he was ours and that as long as he was safe inside me he would continue to live…move…be.

It wasn't easy. When you're pregnant everyone (complete strangers, included) ask when you're due, if you're excited, what names you have picked out and so on. I'd answer that I was due in August, and that his name would be Isaac. Of course our family and close friends knew the situation, but it wasn't something I was prepared to re-hash with just anyone.

I went into labor three days before my due date. I'm one of the few women on the face of the earth that was actually disappointed to know the pregnancy was coming to its natural end. Isaac was born a few short hours later. He was perfect in our eyes and just as precious as any baby could possibly be. He lived for a little over five hours; long enough for Keith and me, along with our parents, to fall completely and forever in love with him. And then he left us.

Two days later at the memorial service, several friends and family members came to love and support us as we said our final goodbyes.

After the last person had left the cemetery, Keith, Dena, and I made our way to the car. Then, Keith gently reminded me that Dena needed diapers and juice. Would I mind if we stopped so he wouldn't have to leave me at the house later?

As I watched the people come and go as if nothing had happened, I was indignant, almost angry – for a moment. And then I realized they were coming and going as if nothing had happened because as far as they knew, nothing had.

"Being a mother is learning about strengths you didn't know you had, and dealing with fears you didn't know existed." ~Linda Wooten

I'll Wait for You

Mie Hansen

The recession hasn't played favorites, very few are safe or exempt from its blows. So when my husband's job as the legal representative for a manufacturing company was eliminated, we packed up and moved back to our home town for him to take over the practice of the one lawyer in our small community. Mr. Savin was retiring and even though it wouldn't be anything exciting or even challenging – wills, real estate transactions, an occasional adoption, a divorce here and there and other routine legal matters, it would provide a steady, secure income for our family. As for me, I could teach music either for the school or give piano, violin and guitar lessons from home.

Both Justin and I had grown up in Morris. Both families still live here, as well as a few of our childhood friends. It wouldn't be so bad. The kids were a bit reluctant, but since they'd spent time here and knew a few of the kids, they weren't too difficult.

The house we ended up buying was one I'd always admired. It was known as the 'Day house'. Ken and Janet Day had built the house in the early fifties when Ken had inherited a large sum of money from an uncle he'd seen only a few times as a child. Their daughter, Lynette, and my mother had been best friends from the time they were in grammar school until Lynette left, the week after they graduated from high school. Mom never heard from her again.

The Day's other child, a son, had been killed in Vietnam a year later. Ken and Janet spent the next several years running the newspaper in Morris and going through the motions of life. But three years ago, they'd sold the paper to a conglomerate and left town. Janet told the ladies in the mid-week Bible study group they were going south to enjoy the sunshine and warm temperatures before they were too old to do so.

The house had been sitting empty since then. So when it went on the market just a week after we started looking, we jumped on it. The rooms were large, it had a sun-room to die for and the thick hand-carved railings and woodwork features were beautiful. Most of the furniture was gone from the house, but there were dishes, lamps, and other items the agent said were part of the deal.

I spent the next few weeks going through everything they'd left; sorting it into 'keep,' 'donate,' and 'toss' piles.

The attic was especially interesting – old Christmas decorations, things from the kids' childhood, Mr. Day's service uniform, Mrs. Day's wedding gown and the letters.

Wrapped inside a quilt in the bottom of a wooden crate was a bundle of letters. Sealed, addressed and stamped, but never opened. The letters were from Bill to Lynette. He was obviously in the military and overseas in Vietnam. Why hadn't they been read? Had they been intercepted? If so, is that why Lynette had left so abruptly?

My curiosity piqued, I learned from my mom and grandma that Bill was Lynette's boyfriend. He was a sweet guy, but the Days didn't think he was good enough for her. They'd secretly planned to run away and get married when he got drafted. When he left, Lynette was sick with worry that he wouldn't come back.

"Why did she leave?"

"Well," Mom hesitated.

"Oh, for goodness sake, Claire," Grandma said, "It was nearly thirty-five years ago."

Looking back at me, she said, "Lynette was pregnant. When Janet found out, she was going to force Lynette to give the baby up for adoption. Lynette was determined to wait for Bill, get married, and raise their baby together."

"Do you know if Lynette and Bill wrote to one another," I asked.

"Lynette wrote Bill every day for the first several months," Mom said. But she never heard from him. At first she thought it was because he couldn't write. Then she got worried that he was one of the POW's or had been killed and was unable to be identified. Then she just gave up. The night before she left, she told me she was going somewhere to decide what she wanted to do about Bill and the baby. I never heard from her again. To my knowledge, no one has."

"What about Bill?"

"He came back looking for her. But she was already gone. The people that lived next door to the Days didn't hide the fact that you could hear them arguing with Bill from their place. He stayed around for a while, worked in the recruiting office over in Newton, I think. And then he was transferred somewhere else and left."

"Why all the questions?"

"Well," I hesitated. "I found something in the attic of the house that might just tell a different story."

Mom wasted no time in tracking down the Days to see if they knew where Lynette was. Hesitant to say much of anything, they finally told Mom they'd not heard from her in over five years, but at the time, she was in Kentucky somewhere.

Mom and Granny spent the next several weeks trying to track down both Lynette and Bill. Just when they were about to give up, Granny ran into Bill's aunt who'd come back to Morris to visit a friend. She told Granny where Bill was living.

Even though Mom and Bill had been friends all through school, she was still nervous about making the call. But, feeling like she owed it to her friends to let them know the truth, she called.

Three days later, Bill was sitting in my living room with the bundle of still unopened letters in his hand and tears running down his face as he listened to Mom telling him about the baby – his and Lynette's baby. He'd never married, but made the Marines his life. He'd just never found anyone that made him forget his first love.

But what about Lynette? We never did find out what happened to her. But Bill's still looking for her and their child.

While my discovery of the letters hasn't ended in the 'happily ever after' I'd originally hoped for, it has given Bill the answers he so desperately needed to make sense of why Lynette hadn't been here when he'd returned. And it's given him a drive and tenacity to do everything possible to find the woman he's loved all these years and the child that is theirs.

As for me, I've learned that people's lives aren't to be treated as pawns in a chess game. It's not for us to decide what's right and wrong, who's good enough and who's not. But instead, we are to love our children unconditionally, and help them make good choices instead of forcing our choices on them.

> *"Good judgment comes from experience, and often experience comes from bad judgment."*
>
> ~Rita Mae Brown

Momma's Sleeping

Tyler Webb

My wife, Annette, and I had married a few weeks after she graduated from high school. I'd been out for two years already, and had a decent job at the local newspaper as the sports photographer. Annette was one of five children and I was one of six, so a large family was something we were both familiar with and wanted. We didn't waste any time, and a week after our first anniversary, we welcomed our little Kathleen into our lives. Over the next nine years we added three boys and one more girl to our clan. Life was busy, but we were happy and healthy. We felt very blessed.

Fast forward three years. I'd been working late, shooting pictures of the high school girl's soccer tournament. When I got home one evening, the kids had been fed an early supper, and Annette was waiting to eat with me. She'd set the table with candles and cloth napkins. My curiosity was definitely piqued, but I couldn't have been more surprised when she handed me a pregnancy test marked positive. Baby number six was on the way. We were thrilled.

The pregnancy was a typical one for Annette with the exception of the dull headaches she had almost daily. The doctor was a bit concerned, and monitored her blood pressure closely. It was a bit on the high side for her, but nothing to be overly concerned about, she said. By the beginning of the eighth month, though, Annette's headaches had subsided and she said she felt better than she had in a long time. Every day was spent playing and reading to the kids, teaching them to pick beans, cucumbers and tomatoes without ruining them and listening to their ideas on what to name the baby sister that would be joining our family in just a few weeks.

One afternoon she called saying I needed to come home from work a bit early to take her to the hospital, it was almost like having our first baby all over again. We were almost giddy with anticipation. It had been a while since we'd had a baby around the house and we were looking forward to experiencing it all again one last time. The delivery was fairly easy and textbook perfect, so to speak. Nothing at all out of the ordinary. In fact, that evening, Annette's folks brought the kids up to meet their new sister, Elise. When I left late that evening, the tired new momma was drifting off to sleep, taking a much-deserved rest before the first of the night's feedings.

Because of the above average work load at home, the doctor kept Annette and Elise in the hospital an extra day to give Annette some rest. But when I did bring them home, it was a wonderful homecoming and I honestly can't remember a day in my life I've been happier or felt more complete. It was absolutely perfect in every way.

In the early morning hours, though, my perfect world took a dive into one of turmoil. Annette woke me up saying she was having the worst headache of her life. She was having trouble seeing and felt as if her head and neck weighed a ton. My instinct told me we needed to act quickly, so phoning Annette's mom and dad, who lived a couple of miles away, I carried Annette to the van, and left for the emergency room as soon as my mother in-law pulled up to the house.

The staff in the ER wasted no time in getting tests started on Annette when they heard her symptoms. Fearing a stroke was imminent; they knew time was of the essence. But before they even had the tests complete, an aneurysm in her brain bled and she was in a coma.

The next few days were a blur of doctors, tests, prayers, tears, and questions left and right from our children. Where was mommy? Why wasn't she taking care of them? Why was 'Grandie' taking care of Elise instead of Mommy? Elise...did she even sense her mommy was gone?

I honestly didn't know which way to turn. Had it not been for our extended family and friends I'm not sure I could have coped. The newspaper was more than generous those first few weeks, allowing me time with my children and my wife.

I could only put the kids off for so long, they wanted and needed to see their mommy. But what do you say when, after being tucked into bed one evening, she disappears?

"Mommy's sleeping," five year old Dillon said.

"Yes," I said, "she's sleeping because she's very sick. She might have to sleep a very long time to get better. So we all need to pray very hard for Mommy and do our very best to take care of each other while she's sick."

Mommy was still sleeping when Elise saw her first Christmas lights a few months later and when her brothers and sisters helped her blow out the single candle on her birthday cake.

Mommy was still sleeping when Kathleen went on her first date and two years after that when she graduated from high school. For five years, Mommy slept.

And then, just as peacefully as she slept, she left us.

In that five years, we'd somehow found our way to a new normal. Our children had to mature a bit faster than most, taking on responsibilities around the house, caring for one another, and visiting their mom in the nursing home even though she didn't know they were there. But they never complained and never stopped loving her. For that I'm thankful.

Three years after Annette died, I met a wonderful woman who lead me to do what I thought I'd never do again…want the love and companionship of a wife. We were married a year later.

In the four years we've been married, she's extended her heart to my children and to Annette's memory as their mother. And when Kathleen and her husband announced a few months ago they were having a baby girl – whose name would be Annette – Lou Ann was the first to say she couldn't think of a better way to honor Annette's memory.

"Life may not be the party we hoped for, but while we're here we should dance." ~Author Unknown

Ivy

Camille Ryan

My mom and dad were almost as happy as I was when Devon asked me to marry him. We'd been dating since our freshmen year of college and he'd been just like another member of the family right from the beginning. It took about twenty four hours for Mom to start talking decorations, guest lists, invitations, and, of course, my wedding gown.

We set the wedding date for June second, the week after finals. We had thought about waiting another year, until we'd graduated, but in the end decided we'd be able to handle senior year better if we weren't trying to plan a wedding at the same time.

"Seven months!" Mom had a moment of panic, but then re-grouped and said we'd be fine.

The day after Christmas, Mom and I went out to scout out all the bargains. We were using yellow and white with gold accents for the wedding; we found gold bows and ribbon to use for decorating and they were on clearance. We wanted to take advantage of the sales. But half way through the morning, Mom started feeling ill, achy and extremely tired.

The next morning, still feeling bad, she thought standing under a hot shower for a while would relieve the aches. But while she was in there, she found a small lump in her breast.

The next few weeks were a blur of MRIs, biopsies, a mastectomy, and consultations. She didn't waste any time getting her shunt put in and starting treatments, determined to be ready for the wedding.

In spite of the effects her chemo had on her, Mom still smiled and got excited whenever she had ideas about flowers, reception table centerpieces, and music. When I would caution her not to do too much, she said the wedding was what kept her going.

By early April it was evident the treatments weren't working. The decision to be made now was whether to continue treatments (which made Mom terribly sick) or to suspend the treatments and keep her comfortable while the cancer ran its course.

"No!" I cried. "Not my mom. I need her. I want her to be a part of my wedding. I want her to see my babies. I want my mom!"

I don't think you ever get too old to need and want your mother. Having my mom was like breathing to me. We'd always been close. We'd had our mom/teenager moments, of course, but not like my friends had with their moms. Even then we'd been able to talk about basically anything.

Three weeks before the wedding, Mom died. On one hand, I was inconsolable, while on the other, I had to be happy she was no longer in pain. She didn't deserve that. But why wasn't I going to get to have my mommy at my wedding?

Several people asked if we planned to go through with the wedding. That thought never really even crossed my mind. My mom had spent so much time and effort to make the day special, even when she didn't feel like lifting her head off the pillow, I wouldn't have even thought to let her down by letting all her hard work go to waste.

The day of the wedding arrived. My bridesmaids and I were all getting ready, my mom's absence painfully obvious. The girls were trying so hard to keep it together for my sake, but they'd all known Mom. And then in came Molly.

My Aunt Molly was the youngest of Mom's three sisters. She'd planned on coming to the wedding, of course, but my grandma, who is in a nursing home, was having a hard time dealing with Mom's death. She was refusing to eat and being difficult to care for, so Aunt Molly was worried about traveling from Kentucky to Virginia in case something happened with Gram. But now, here she was.

"Aunt Molly! I didn't think you were coming. Did something happen to Gram?" I was almost scared to ask.

"No, honey, she's fine. In fact, she's the reason I'm here. When she found out I had decided not to come she got downright angry with me. She said I had to be here – that you couldn't get married without this."

As she was talking, Aunt Molly was pulling some long strands of English ivy wrapped in moist toweling from a bag.

"Where's your bouquet, Cammie?"

"Over there in the box. But, what's that?"

"It's ivy. But it's not just any ivy. You know the big plant Gram has?"

"Yes, she's had it forever. I remember her fussing about it going with her when she moved to the nursing home."

"Yes, well, it turns out she started that plant with ivy she pulled out of your mom's bridal bouquet. Gram said it was hard enough you having to face the day without Sandy here to share it with you. She wanted you to have some of this to put in your bouquet so you'd have a part of her happiness with you on your wedding day."

That's all it took. The tears started flowing and none of us even attempted to stop them. It would have been useless. Dad came in to say it was time to begin and wasn't sure what to think. But when we told him, he smiled; tears spilling out of his eyes.

"Well, okay, then. It's time for your mom and I to walk you down the aisle. Let's go start the rest of your life."

"There are things that we don't want to happen but have to accept, things we don't want to know but have to learn, and people we can't live without but have to let go." ~Author Unknown

Keeping a Positive Attitude

Sing Your Heart Out
Mark Rickerby

The longer I live, the more I realize
That all the favorite subjects of poets –
The moon, the wind, the stars,
The seasons, the clouds and flowers,
The human heart,
And all the thoughts and feelings
That crowd our minds –
Are nothing more
Than a reflection of ourselves;
A reflection that changes
From moment to moment.

Have you ever been sad on a sunny day?
Did it matter that the sun was shining?

Have you ever felt so spiritually desolate

That you resented happiness in others?

Pain feeds on itself.

But . . .
Have you ever been happy and noticed
How friendly everyone else seemed to be?
How all the street lights changed for you?
How even animals came bounding over
And every flower leaned in your direction
As if to taste a little of your essence?

It had nothing to do with them.

It's a great mystery.
We see the world as we are,
As we feel,
And the world seems to know it.
There are many types of consciousness
Beneath the surface we can see.

Love is no different.
We give up on it,

Not the other way around.

Love will never knock at a hermit's door.

To the embittered and distrustful,

Love is like an eager customer

With pockets full of cash

Peering through the window of a closed shop.

The cure is simple.

We must open the doors,

Pull back the curtains,

Clean the place up,

And turn on all the lights

So nobody passing will say,

"Oh, it must be closed."

We must be willing to take another chance.

Yes, the great, mad spectacle of life

May have pain as well as pleasure,

Sadness as well as joy,

But never taking part in it is worse.

It's better to sing your heart out

And receive a few bad reviews

Than to never know how it feels

To sing your heart out.

Heartache isn't the worst fate, dear friend.

Emptiness is.

"To succeed in life, you need three things: a wishbone, a backbone and a funnybone."

~Reba McEntire

Be Stubborn; Be Strong

Diana M. Amadeo

Today, I stand on my own two feet. My shaky hands are calm enough to play the piano again. Tucked away in storage are canes, Lofstrand crutches, wheelchairs, a motorized scooter and power chair for mobilization. That was my plight with multiple sclerosis. Then, destiny seemed bleak. My family and I were resigned to "prepare for the worst yet hope for the best."

My husband came home from work a dozen years ago to find me extremely ill. That morning it was thought I had a virus. But what he found on homecoming was not someone with the flu. Instead, his wife was semi coherent, blind, and partially deaf with weakness on the left side of her body.

Later, in the hospital, after C scans, a spinal tap, and MRIs revealed many sclerotic brain and spinal lesions, doctors confirmed the diagnosis of multiple sclerosis. I listened to their revelation of doom, but didn't react. As soon as they left, in the privacy of the hospital room, I cried. I stumbled and felt my way alone to the bathroom. I didn't want anyone's help.

A thousand miles away my mother heard of my plight and called the hospital. "I heard you are being stubborn and refuse to use a walker," she said, barely audible.

I debated hanging up the phone. Instead, I listened.

"Keep being stubborn," my mother said. "Be strong. It will get you through this."

My blindness subsided quickly into double vision. The doctors couldn't promise that my vision would ever be normal, but within several months it was. My hearing also improved, but never regained its prior clarity. Physical therapy got me moving again, but weakness, spasticity and tremors left me dependent on crutches or wheelchairs. Then there were bladder problems, fatigue, and deep depression issues. Hopes faded into disappointment with each medication failure.

Every move, action, and thought required Herculean efforts. Morning activities of daily living left afternoon exhaustion. Days passed. Soon my health stabilized to a routine of a few hours of wheelchair/Lofstrand crutch activities in the mornings; afternoon respite and evening lethargy. This was my new normal. Our busy family life continued. My three children had to grow up very quickly and assume responsibilities none of their friends had.

The days turned into weeks then years in this fashion. We trudged on, doing the very best that we could. After a decade, each day was exhausting, but routine. I kept my mother's advice. I was stubbornly strong.

Despite years of seemingly little progress, I persevered with daily 20 minutes of walking treadmill, medication, upper body exercise, a healthy diet, meditation, and rest. Somewhere into the tenth year of little progress with MS, I noticed rest periods were less frequent. My head seemed clearer. My speech was sharper and clearer. I put away the ambulation assistance.

Repeat MRI's showed that my lesions still existed but their signals were less intense (less active). My doctor was amazed. I am excited and grateful to this very day. Do I still feel MS symptons? Yes, every day. The little reminders of spasms, gimpy legs, weakness, and fatigue still sideline me a few hours each day. Cognitive impairment sometimes makes me seem older than I am. But my attitude is good. It's true that I still move a little slow, sometimes take a few minutes to say the right words. I also require daily rest periods. But I'm not suffering. Diligence and hard work yielded a deep appreciation of life. A hard day is beautiful; rain, snow, sleet, or sunshine. I'm off all my medication (although they are standby in my medicine cabinet) and I focus on life's positives; I acknowledge and then let go of the negatives. Life's not always easy, but my life now is light-years better than before.

Is this change just a lull or remission in the disease process? Perhaps. But without being stubborn and strong willed, I wouldn't have exercised and thus had the muscular ability to get to this level, again. I wouldn't have developed the positive self talk if instead I had wallowed in depression and self pity. Who knows how I would be if not for my mother's words years ago?

Leave it to Mom to deliver the best advice I've ever received.

"Oh, my friend, it's not what they take away from you that counts. It's what you do with what you have left." ~Hubert Humphrey

You're Not Lost Until You Are Out Of Gas

Bob Janet

When I turned 16 years old, my parents gave me my first car and said two things.

1. Drive as far as you like without gas, but never drive an inch without oil. Back in the 1960s, cars burnt oil that needed to be constantly replaced and driving a motor vehicle without oil would destroy the motor.

2. "You're not lost until you are out of gas."

Little did I know that this second bit of advice would serve me so well. It was years later that I realized they were not just talking about operating an automobile.

In 1970, I joined the family retail and wholesale business full time. We owned and operated a tire retread shop and an electronics store. We were on the verge of adding the area's biggest appliance business in the summer of 1972 when a hurricane named Agnes decided to settle in the skies over central Pennsylvania.

We were informed by the national flood warning system that our business property could receive two to three feet of water within the next twelve hours. We did not panic; we had been through high water and floods before. We immediately prepared for the onslaught Mother Nature was bringing.

Knowing that weather forecasting is not an exact science, Dad decided to play it safe and had us move every piece of merchandise and machinery onto six-foot high platforms.

That included our brand new, two million dollar retread tire shop for which we owed the bank. We felt we were ready for whatever Mother Nature had in store for us.

Sure enough, there were miscalculations by the weather forecasting people. Twenty-four hours and nine feet of floodwaters later, we watched from a hill a quarter mile away as our building was ripped apart and every piece of equipment and merchandise floated away.

In less than a half hour we had lost our entire business. The tire retread shop, tire inventory, electronics inventory, displays, and every building had sustained major damage, including the newly constructed building that was to be our new appliance store in three weeks. We lost everything. For the first time in my life, I felt what LOST really meant.

The next day, as the water receded and we were better able to survey our losses, we discovered for certain that we had lost *everything*. Even the big, six-foot tall safe that took six men to move was gone. All lost. As he walked away, my father only said, "Stop up at the house later this evening."

Later that evening, I went to my parents' house. As I got out of the car, I was wondering what my father would do now to make a living. We not only lost everything in the flood, but everything we had lost was mortgaged against our homes and we had no way of making the payments. We owed the bank over two million dollars. I thought my only salvation was to go back into the teaching I did before I went into business with my parents.

My father was sitting at the kitchen table with a tablet, busily writing. As I sat down next to him he asked, "Why are you so gloomy?"

I replied, "We just lost everything! How are you going to make a living?"

He stood up and said, "I'm going back in business. Aren't you?"

I replied, "How? We lost everything and we owe over two million dollars. How are we going to keep our houses?"

He smiled, "You're not lost until you are out of gas." I asked him what that meant, and he told me I would figure it out.

Dad told me he would make arrangements to have new retread equipment, new tire inventory, and new electronic merchandise delivered by the weekend. We would sell from under tents and out of trailers until we repaired or built new buildings. I was to go to the bank the next morning and borrow two million dollars. I remember going home that night and my wife Jan asked me what my father had said. When I told her we were going back in business, she asked me how. I told her, "Dad said we are not lost until we are out of gas." She asked what that meant, and I replied, "I don't know, but I have to figure it out by morning."

The next day I went to the bank and as I approached the president, he was very solemn. The first thing he said was, "Looks like we have a bad situation here, Bob." As I started to tell him how we were going back in business under tents and out of trailers, he became more positive. When he looked me in the eye and said, "Tell me more," I realized what my father meant by "You are not lost until you are out of gas."

We had lost our equipment, our merchandise, and our buildings. Mother Nature had taken about everything we had. I realized the one thing that cannot be taken from me under any circumstance is my talent for selling. I didn't have buildings. I didn't have any merchandise, but I still had my talent for selling.

I made the biggest sale I had ever made. I sold the bank on the idea that if they did not loan us two million dollars more, even though we had little or no collateral, they would never get back any of the money we owed them. I used my selling talents to secure enough capital to rebuild and restock. My father used his selling talents to convince all of our suppliers to send not only merchandise but also trailers, and to give us extended, free financing terms.

Five days after the floodwaters receded, we were back in business. We were soon retreading and selling tires. I started a flood sale and had the best quarter ever in electronic sales. We received the appliances on the date we had planned and had the grand opening sale for our new appliance store as scheduled – under a tent.

No matter how difficult are the circumstances that you face in business and life, no matter how devastating your setback is, no matter what they take away from you, they cannot take your talents. If your talents are not up to date – learn new ones. Your talents will always be the gas in your personal tank and, "You're not lost until you are out of gas."

"What counts is not necessarily the size of the dog in the fight - it's the size of the fight in the dog".

- Dwight D. Eisenhower

Rock-a-Hoola Dreams

Mark Rickerby

There once was a glorious place in the desert
Right smack in the middle of Death Valley.
It was called The Rock-a-Hoola Water Park.
And brother, that place was right up my alley.

It was a virtual oasis of wholesome family fun
Where bright, turquoise-green water flowed.
The laughter of children filled the air above it
As the rivers washed away the dust of the road.

Happy Rock 'n Roll music from a simpler time
Still played there, as if not a year had gone by.
It was a place parents could trust with their kids.
As American as baseball and mom's apple pie.

Sadly, the Rock-a-Hoola Water Park is no more.
The doors are closed and the bright rivers are dry.
Music and laughter no longer flood from the gate.
No water beckons the road-weary traveling by.

I left the highway and stood at the rusty gate.
It squeaked mournfully in the hot desert air.
The contrast between what it was and is now
Made me think of the man who'd built it there.

He manifested his dream right out of the sand.
And the dream came true – for a while anyway.
But the dream died and now lies abandoned.
There is nowhere left for the children to play.

That's what bothered me the most, of course,
But its closing bugged me metaphorically, too.
You see, that water park glistening in the sun
Represented anything great that we try to do.

Our dreams are as bright as that shining oasis.
The water – our desire to make them come true.
The desert – the world, full of fear and doubt.
The rocky sand a delicate flower grows through.

But I don't want to live a life without dreams;
A boat meant for the sea, yet never embarks.
And I don't want to spend my life in a world

Without shimmering Rock-a-Hoola Water Parks.

So if your eyes have lost the long-ago sparkle
Of a soft dream you imagined way back when,
Open the gate for business, repaint the old sign,
And let the waters of desire flow freely again.

"Life is a great big canvas, and you should throw all the paint on it you can." ~Danny Kaye

Weakness or Strength?

Author Unknown

Sometimes your biggest weakness can become your biggest strength. Take, for example, the story of one ten-year-old boy who decided to study judo despite the fact he had lost his left arm in a devastating car accident.

The boy began lessons with an old Japanese judo master. The boy was doing well, so he couldn't understand why, after three months of training the master had taught him only one move.

"Sensei," the boy finally said, "Shouldn't I be learning more moves?"

"This is the only move you know, but this is the only move you'll ever need to know," the sensei replied.

Not quite understanding, but believing in his teacher, the boy kept training.

Several months later, the sensei took the boy to his first tournament. Surprising himself, the boy easily won his first two matches. The third match proved to be more difficult, but after some time, his opponent became impatient and charged. The boy deftly used his one move to win the match. Still amazed by his success, the boy was now in the finals.

This time, his opponent was bigger, stronger, and more experienced. For a while, the boy appeared to be overmatched. Concerned that the boy might get hurt, the referee called a time-out. He was about to stop the match when the sensei intervened.

"No," the sensei insisted, "let him continue."

Soon after the match resumed, his opponent made a critical mistake — he dropped his guard. Instantly, the boy used his move to pin him. The boy had won the match and the tournament. He was the champion.

On the way home, the boy and sensei reviewed every move in each and every match. Then the boy summoned the courage to ask what was really on his mind.

"Sensei, how did I win the tournament with only one move?"

"You won for two reasons," the sensei answered. "First, you've almost mastered one of the most difficult throws in all of judo. And second, the only known defense for that move is for your opponent to grab your left arm."

The boy's biggest weakness had become his biggest strength.

"Life is what we make it, always has been, always will be." ~Grandma Moses

The Tips of the Tallest Trees

Mark Rickerby

After years of writing poetry
and struggling to break free,
I found the perfect metaphor
for all I want to be.

It came to me by accident,
as good things often do,
and my task now, as a poet,
is to tell the tale to you.

I was feeling tired and beaten,
worn-out and weary to the bone.
I hadn't left the house in days,
shut off from the world, alone.

When something deep inside me said,
"That's enough! Get out of bed!
Stop feeling sorry for yourself
or you're as good as dead!"

After being buried in despair so long,
I wondered from where this voice had risen.
It was like a visit from a long-lost friend
after many hopeless years in prison.

So I opened up the dusty curtains
and let the bright sunlight flood in.
And as every poet will attest –
when one looks out, one looks within.

The street outside was bustling.
Lovers laughed and children played.
And I couldn't help but realize
how far from life I'd strayed.

My world seemed so dark and small
next to the one I saw outside.
In a moment, I felt all I'd lost.
The dam broke and I cried.

I knew I had to find a way
to purge this sadness from my soul,
dust myself off, rejoin the living,

and make my fractured spirit whole.

So I splashed my face and went outside.
It was a beautiful, windy day
but my heart ached with melancholy
that just would not go away.

I walked and walked for hours
like a tortured, restless ghost
for when we confront our demons,
that's when they attack the most.

I don't know how much time had passed
when I reached the base of a hill.
Determined to walk the pain away,
I pressed on further still.

I have always loved to climb
because of how it clears the mind
but I had no peace within that day
so what peace could I hope to find?

I remembered an old line I heard once

and it rang in my ears from the start . . .
"You won't find your heart in a temple
if there's no temple in your heart."

I've never been a very faithful man.
I never found answers in a church.
I didn't know what I was looking for.
I only knew I had to search.

I climbed until my muscles ached,
not even sure what I was proving
or what I was running to or from.
I just had to keep on moving.

I was thoroughly exhausted
when I finally reached the top
but I saw a taller hill beyond
and my soul wouldn't let me stop.

I suppose I was tired of quitting,
of feeling beaten, small and weak.
I couldn't let myself give up
until I reached the highest peak.

These were not just hills.
They were everything I'd ever tried.
They were every half-accomplished goal
begging fulfillment, deep inside.

Many of my tears, that day,
mingled with the dusty soil.
The hills had come to represent
a lifetime's travail and toil.

I cried for all the love I'd lost
and for all the wasted years.
I cried for every broken dream
on this, my trail of tears.

I finally reached the second peak,
so high, I felt like I was flying
or I could reach up and touch heaven.
The howling wind was like God sighing.

I was now the highest living thing
but for the tips of the tallest trees,

pitching and swaying magnificently
in the gentle Autumn breeze.

The stars were beginning to twinkle
as the fiery sun set in the west.
I lay down in a bed of leaves
to grant myself some rest.

And when I looked up to the sky
framed by the towering trees,
a strange quiet filled my soul
and this thought came to me . . .

The trees, though firmly rooted,
never stop reaching for the sky.
They don't worry about what falls away
or how fast the years pass by.

They don't complain about the weather
or struggle against ferocious winds
yet they're still standing proudly
when the calm returns again.

This is a very, very old idea.
It did not begin with me.
A poet once said she'd never see
a poem as lovely as a tree.

And I hate to repeat an old cliché
but truth always stays the same
though it comes from many places
and travels under many names.

I'd heard this philosophy so often,
I considered it "nickel and dime"
but on this strange and soulful day,
it was like I'd heard it the first time.

A poet lives on metaphors.
They're his lifeblood, you see.
So I was happy to truly discover
the ancient lesson of the tree.

To stop fighting and agree with life
and whatever it happens to bring,
for a soul tormented by loss and pain

can never learn to dance or sing.

To have a strong foundation
while always reaching out.
To keep growing, no matter what.
That's what life's about.

These strong and noble giants
whispered a message for me to keep
and under their sheltering canopy,
I slowly drifted off to sleep.

I awoke to a bright, new morning
and made my way back down the hill
and everywhere a tear had fallen,
a flower stood, serene and still.

I looked back up to the hilltop once
to that place where every tree's a poem,
said thank you, then turned and smiled
and, peacefully, headed home.

"The greatest oak was once a little nut who held its ground." ~Author Unknown

In It for Life

Aubrette Benoit

I was looking forward to the weekend. I'd be taking my daughter and traveling up state to celebrate my grandparents' sixtieth anniversary with family and friends. It would be the first time for most of the family to see Portia since she'd been born seven months ago. And it was always good to see Grandpa and Nanna. The only thing that would make the weekend less than what it might be was that Samuel wasn't going with us.

When we'd gotten married five years ago, I would have bet my life that nothing would ever come between us. I would have lost that bet.

Portia had been a surprise. We'd not completely decided to have children. But when I found I was pregnant, I looked at it as having our minds made up for us. Samuel didn't see it like that at all.

He barely looked at the ultrasound pictures the doctor gave me and any time I suggested a name, he'd say, "Whatever you like will be fine."

He wouldn't attend birthing classes, saying he wasn't going to sit in a room full of pregnant women listening to them breathe and hiss. I wasn't going by myself to have everyone giving me pity looks, so I rented DVDs and watched them by myself at home.

I was confused, angry, and hurt by his lack of enthusiasm. But I was even more hurt and angry at his lack of care about my feelings, not to mention my health and safety, and that of our child. Would he even have time to take me to the hospital?

I felt my first contractions as we were getting ready to go to bed, but didn't say a word. But by three o'clock in the morning, I knew I needed to say something; that we'd need to go to the hospital soon.

When we arrived and were settled into a room, he actually seemed somewhat concerned when my contractions began to get really intense. But when I was in the final stages of labor, he acted as though I was embarrassing him.

I fell in love with Portia Jeanette the moment she was placed in my arms. Samuel, on the other hand, wouldn't hold her. What was wrong with him?

For the last seven months he'd done little to help out and I could count on both hands the times he'd held his daughter. I tried talking to him, but he'd shut down saying he was fine; that the baby didn't need anything from him.

I told Samuel I was going to stay a couple of extra days to spend time with my mom and sister. I said that when I got back he needed to be able to tell me if the way things were now was the way they were going to be. And if they were, then I wouldn't stay in the marriage.

I loved Samuel, but I couldn't live like we'd been living. And I didn't want Portia to grow up in a home where one of her parents clearly didn't want her.

Being with my family made me realize how tense I'd been since I'd gotten pregnant. Worrying about Samuel and trying to make things good had taken its toll. It was so refreshing to smile and laugh and have others take joy in my daughter's sweetness. Maybe we would be better off without Samuel.

The anniversary party was filled with laughter and conversations with family and friends I'd not seen in quite some time. As part of the festivities, my mom and her brothers and sister had put together a slide show of pictures from my grandparents' youth all the way to the present. Instead of music in the background of the presentation, there were the voices of my grandparents, recalling both the good and bad times that had made their marriage what it was. My grandfather had served in Vietnam and was gone when their second child was born. They'd weathered financial hardships, the death of one of their children and two grandchildren, heart attacks and other health concerns, and the not-so-joyous things that come with getting older. But, they said, they'd done it together because they'd said 'for richer or poorer, sickness and in health…' They said team work, that's what it took to make it work. And while they hadn't won every game, they'd played it to the end – together.

I knew then that's what I had to try to do, become a team again – me, Samuel and Portia Jeanette. I just hoped it wasn't too late and that Samuel still wanted to be on it.

Portia and I arrived home a few hours before Samuel was due back from work. I dressed us both in our nicest dresses and set the table with cloth napkins, candle light, and our favorite Italian take-out. When he arrived home, he was surprised and even though he tried to hide it, I saw the smile tugging at the corners of his mouth when he saw Portia smiling at him in her highchair.

"Samuel," I said, "I want us to be a family – all three of us. Portia needs and deserves our love and the very best we can give her. And we deserve to be happy as a family and as a couple."

Samuel looked away, but I could see the tears in his eyes. I laid my hand on his shoulder and asked him to please tell me what was wrong. I told him if there was any hope for us at all I had to know.

Samuel broke down in tears telling me how much he loved me and our precious daughter. He said that he'd kept his distance because he was afraid of what would happen if he got too close.

Samuel had told me early on in our relationship that his younger brother died as a baby. But what he'd not told me was that he believed he killed him. He'd been six at the time and playing on the floor beside his brother who was lying on a blanket batting at his portable mobile. He'd accidentally knocked his Leggo tower over on the baby's head. About a week later his little brother died. And he was afraid it was his fault.

Samuel's mom had told me the baby had died of SIDS. It's a tragedy with no real known cause or cure, but it certainly wasn't the result of a few Leggos on the head. As I tried to console Samuel, he said he knew in his head what I was saying was right, but in his heart, he wasn't so sure. He'd never been able to convince himself beyond a doubt that he'd not played a part in his baby brother's death.

We talked long into the night. Samuel confessed that he was scared to be with Portia because he didn't want anything to happen to her. But he assured me that he loved her with all his heart.

That's all I needed to hear. Not caring that I might 'pay for it' the next day, I went to Portia's crib and brought her to her daddy. When I placed her sleeping body in his arms, he held her close and kept saying over and over, "I'm so sorry, precious baby, I'm so sorry."

As a family we went to see a counselor weekly for about six months to help Samuel work through his fears and deep-seated feelings of guilt. But the morning Samuel said he'd take Portia to the doctor with what was obviously an ear ache, I knew we were going to be fine.

> "Continuity gives us roots; change gives us branches, letting us stretch and grow and reach new heights." ~Pauline R. Kezer

On Looking Through Old Photographs
Mark Rickerby

Sometimes the heart doesn't know it needs healing.
Sometimes the soul just gets used to the pain.
And the path which once shone so brightly before us
Withers so slowly we barely notice the change.

For not every dream of the past can come with us.
Not every wish is meant to come true.
A whole lot of living and loving and losing
Goes into the making of a me and a you.

Not till we're filled can we know we were hollow.
We must cure our own blindness before we can see.
No one's born with wisdom, talent, or virtue.
We must conquer ourselves to be all we can be.

It's not just our triumphs that shape and define us.
It's our failures and fears and shortcomings, too.
Not till our hearts have been broken and empty
Can we savor the time when they're happy and full.

We all dream of happiness, of fortune and fame
And in the races we run, we all want to be first
But the fact is we learn most quickly and deeply
When our lives are in ruin and the pain is the worst.

So don't regret yesterday for all of its sorrows.
Don't fret for the dark times when you lost your way.
Don't put yourself down for mistakes of the past
For they gave you the insights that you have today.

The path of today is always in our keeping
And yesterday's needn't be utterly lost.
A few dreams survive if only we'll tend them.
The bridge between then and now can be crossed!

"The gem cannot be polished without friction nor man without trials." ~Confucius

Gratitude

Mark Rickerby

Poets, it seems, are often too dismal,
as if life and all in it were truly abysmal.
I too often strive to soothe worries with rhyme,
dwelling on sorrows and the passage of time.
When there's so much to celebrate, to chance and explore!
Seems very ungrateful to wish there was more.
Say I wrote all my troubles, one by one, in a row.
How much further the list of my blessings would go!
Just look at this glorious Eden we live in.
Can you think of one thing we haven't been given?
Miraculous! Perfect! Not one thing is wrong.
Still, men find every reason to not get along.
We have moonlight and sunsets and rainbows and flowers.
Deep, starry nights and bright, happy sun showers.
Wondrous creatures, every kind, shape, and size.
Birds singing to greet us each day when we rise.
Such wonder and mystery without and within.
Well, I'm too full of love to hold it all in.
My heart feels as though it may split at the seams.
It can barely contain all my plans, hopes, and dreams.

I'm completely astonished, awakened and free.
I'm everything that life should be!

I climb up a mountain to breathe in the air
and leave behind, with each step, one more useless care.
The sun ripples like laughter across the wide sea.
I smile at a flower; it smiles back at me.
The wind lifts a scent from the meadow below
and reminds me of the first girl I kissed, long ago.
I kneel in the clover, feel my spirit expand.
A bright butterfly stops to rest on my hand.
The clouds, ever present, yet no two the same,
give lively imaginations to a game.
"Look! A sailboat! A rabbit! An angel! A swan!"
And it's the best kind of game because no one's ever wrong.

Everyone should have a special place like my hill
just to rest and let the mind roam free where it will.
Far away from the traffic, the noise and the dust
in the crystal clear sunshine of a world they can trust.
Life's easy to master when we strive not to worry
and snatch up the whip from the cruel hand of hurry.
When we stop struggling to accumulate more than we need

for the god with the insatiable appetite – greed.
You can't take it with you. That old line is true.
And you know, when it's all said and done, we won't want to.
For when our old, mortal husks fall away and are buried,
all we'll need is the goodness and love that they carried.
So relax into life, breathe deep and let go.
Attain what you need but don't sell your soul.
For it's a treasure far beyond the mere baubles of men
and once lost, much harder to earn back again.

Just a few thoughts from my heart to yours
hoping that one or maybe two will endure
to make some dreary day a little bit brighter
and the load that you carry, perhaps, a bit lighter.
Though the author claims no special wisdom or power
to lecture from atop some ivory tower.
I'm just one more soul, no different from you,
whose made all the mistakes and a few new ones, too.
But somehow survived all those nights without end,
my tired, tattered spirit refusing to mend,
wondering what so much pain could be for,
the spiritual carnage of a personal war.

For it's in punishing ourselves that we can be most unkind
and the most torn, fearful battles take place in the mind.
But the hardest climb leads to the best, brightest view
so this is my humble message to you,
like a bottle set adrift on some far, lonesome shore,
from my small, solitary island to yours . . .

Though we may never meet, we are friends through this poem.
In this way, we can never be truly alone.
For though we're apart in time, place and name,
we are joined in the same, sanctified mortal game.
We may differ in doctrine, language and race
but in the most sacred ways, we have perfect grace.
We both dream and love. We both bleed and cry.
And as sure as we're living, we someday must die.
So now, while the grapes are plump on the vine,
take time to laugh and savor the wine.
Turn your heart to the beauty that's in and around you.
Walk gently, with love, and the same will surround you.
You'll surely see further the farther you go.
And remember – it's pain which helps us to grow.
For with all of its sadness, its heartache and strife,

with all of its sorrow, it's a wonderful life.

Yes, with all of its sorrow, it's a wonderful life.

"As we express our gratitude, we must never forget
that the highest appreciation is not
to utter words, but to live by them."
~John Fitzgerald Kennedy

****

We hope you enjoyed reading
Life Freshly Squeezed.

Remember to come visit us at
www.LifeFreshlySqueezed.com for more
information about our upcoming books
and how your story can become part of our
project to make the world a better place.

Our Family of Contributors

Betty R. Cornett – Wife, mother, and part-time writer from Chattanooga, TN. She enjoys running, reading, knitting, and her retirement. She can be reached via email at bcornett1@mail.com.

Maureen Perry – Living in Bangor, ME, and teaches 3rd graders. Very active in her church and likes to travel when she can.

Adam Henderson – He is a former attorney and resides in Richardson, TX. He enjoys spending time with his kids and grandkids. He also, enjoys hunting, fishing and writing.

Diana M. Amadeo – Lives in Merrimack, NH and is a multi-award winning author who has 500 + publications with her byline in books, anthologies, magazines, newspapers, and online. She can be reached via email at da.author@comcast.net

Ellen Hines – Ellen owns her own advertising company in Sunnyvale, CA when she lives with her husband and kids. She has written numerous articles on various topics. Ellen can be reached at ellensh@adexec.com.

Rebecca Carr – She currently resides in Denver, CO and is working in the resort industry. She loves to spend her free time curled up on her sofa and writing.

Suzanne Kunze – She is a freelance writer living in Holland, MI. She runs writing workshops from home. Susanne can be emailed at suzannekunze@yahoo.com.

Lillie Shockney – Resides in Reisterstown, MD, and she is an Administrative Director and Associate Professor at John's Hopkins University. Lillie is a published author and nationally recognized public speaker on the subject of breast cancer. She has written 13 books and more then 200 articles on this subject. Her complete bio can be found at http://www.hopkinsmedicine.org/avon_foundation_breast_center/team_approach/our_team/leadership/lillie_shockney.html.

Candice Becker – Candice has found her bliss in moving back to her home town in Cedar Rapids, IA. She enjoys spending her time with her friends, her church and her dog.

Blake O'Shea – Blake lives in New York City and runs his own music school. Writing is his other love and gives him the escape from the stress of city life.

Cassy Fox – She is now living on her own little farm in Virginia. She raises horses, chickens, and her kids.

Marlene Andreasen – Marlene's true passion in photography. She is a photographer for a local newspaper and magazine in San Diego, CA. She can be reached via email at marlene.andreasen@yahoo.com

Mara Suranno – Mara has found that writing has become her true love since an accident has placed her in a wheelchair. She currently lives in San Francisco, CA

Linette Boisvert – She is enjoying life as a social worker with her family in Portland, OR

Misty Mills – Misty still lives in North Carolina where she spends her leisure time writing for several online magazines and runs her own blog. She can be emailed at millsmedia@writeme.com.

Francine Jacobs – Francine recently received her Masters Degree in Journalism. She enjoys "writing, reading running and raising Rottweilers".

Russell Johnson – Is a business instructor at a small community college and resides in Ephraim, Utah. He can be reached via email at russ.johnson@snow.edu

Norman Mitchell – Along with sharing a large ranch with five generations of family in Montana, writing makes his life complete.

Patricia Rogowski – New York City is where Pat and her family call home. She is a co-owner of a restaurant and tavern. Rollerblading in Central Park makes life complete.

Melissa Row – Mellissa works for an advertising company in Chicago, IL. She is a writer, photographer, and researcher. She can be reached at mtrow@gmail.com.

Grace Williamson – Grace lives with her husband and kids in Nashville, TN. She is a children's story and song writer.

Linda Harrop – She resides in San Diego, CA, where she owns and operates a boat rental business with one of her daughters.

Tim Nelson – Tim is a pastoral counselor in private practice in Portland, OR. He runs humanitarian missions to third world countries. He can be reached at tim.nelson99@yahoo.com.

Janet Evans – Janet is a travel writer living in Miami, FL. She also raises French Poodles.

Belle M. DuCharme - Belle DuCharme is a self employed Dental Business Consultant, writer, and speaker who lives and works in San Diego, CA. She can be emailed at belle@topspeak.net.

Mae Baas – Mae is a private duty nurse living in Las Vegas, NV. She enjoys writing and hot air ballooning.

Leah Weissmuller – Leah owns and operates a small retail clothing store in Dallas, TX. She is currently studying for her MBA degree in business. She can be emailed at lweissmuller@bigstring.com.

Emily Murphy – She is retired and living in St. Paul, MN where she runs a small online business where she sells hand made jewelry. Emily can be reached at emurph@gmail.com.

Millie Gaulin - Writing has been Millie's way of getting through all the rainy days living in Seattle, WA. She also teaches square dancing to area residents.

Jackie Tucker – Jackie currently resides in Little Rock, AR with her family. She is working as a floral designer for a local florist.

Mark Rickerby - Mark Rickerby is a writer, songwriter and singer residing in Burbank, CA. For information about his published works and current projects, visit www.markrickerby.com.

Abbie Donnelly – Abbie works for a dental lab based in Cleveland, OH. She loves writing and is currently working on her own romance novel.

Teresa Perry – Teresa is a teacher for special needs kids in the Charlotte, NC area. She loves taking her Scottish terrier with her to local nursing homes as a canine companion and reading to the residents.

Emma Skov – Emma lives in Sacramento, CA, and is fluent in five languages. She translates corporate documents for several corporations based in Northern California. Emma can be reached at skovemma@yahoo.com.

Jodie Cox – Jodie is now living her life out of an RV. She and her husband travel the US taking photographs and selling them to various vendors.

Theresa Carpenter – Theresa lives and works in a bookstore in Richmond, VA. She will be beginning her longtime dream of going to school to be a veterinarian. She can be reached via email at tcarpenter144@gmail.com.

Linda Davis – She lives in New York City and works with her husband in a private detective agency. Writing has been a lifelong passion and she is working on her own crime novel.

Valerie Mayville – Valerie runs an artist studio in Raleigh, NC. Aside from art, she enjoys writing and making items out of stained glass.

Nate Mailey – Nate is a musician and songwriter who lives in Los Angles, CA. He performs with his band at several local entertainment venues. Nate can be contacted at natemailey@rocketmail.com.

Logan Preston – Logan lives in the Philadelphia area and designs women's apparel for various boutique clothing shops. He is working on starting his own clothing line very soon.

Olivia Strong – Olivia is living in New Brunswick, NJ where she is pursuing her degree in psychology. She also volunteers helping underprivileged children.

Agathe Girard - She is happily spending her retirement years with her husband in Provo, UT. She likes to get up early to read and write while her husband goes fishing or hunting. Aggie can be reached at agathegirard@ymail.com.

Olivia Middleton – Olivia lives in Boston, MA, where she volunteers her time helping women who have been the victim of physical or sexual abuse. She is a paraplegic, but she enjoys competing in wheelchair races and marathons.

Mie Hansen – Mie is currently living in St. Louis, MO. She is a private chef and enjoys travel and playing her guitar. Mie can be contacted at miehansen55@yahoo.com.

Tyler Webb – Tyler runs his own telemarketing company in Atlanta, GA He enjoys riding his motorcycle and golf when he can find the time.

Camille Ryan – She is living in Arlington, VA and works as a bookkeeper in an accounting office. She is active in her church choir and enjoys knitting.

Bob Janet – He lives in Matthews, NC, and has been owner and operator of a Retail, Wholesale, Service and Manufacturing business for more than forty-five years. Bob can be reached at Bob@BobJanet.com.

Aubrette Benoit – Aubrette is a freelance writer who lives in Portland, ME. She enjoys the blessings of her children, grandchildren, and life in general.

www.ingramcontent.com/pod-product-compliance
Lightning Source LLC
Chambersburg PA
CBHW060820050426
42453CB00008B/517